Only Jesus of Nazareth
Can Sit on The Throne of David

John P. McTernan

Additional Books By John McTernan

God's Final Warning to America
Israel: The Blessing or the Curse
Father Forgive Them

Only Jesus of Nazareth Series:
Only Jesus of Nazareth Can be
Israel's King Messiah
Only Jesus of Nazareth Can Sit
on The Throne of David

John McTernan may be reach by email at:
McT911@aol.com

or visit his website at:
www.branchofdavid.org

write:
John McTernan
PO Box 444,
Liverpool, PA 17045

Dedication

This book is dedicated to my friend Fred Peipman. Fred has been such a faithful friend. His wisdom and insight in the Scriptures have been such a blessing. His support and prayers were always there when I needed them.

Table of Contents

Foreword

This book is the second in the Only Jesus of Nazareth series. It is a compilation of my work in a previous series called King Messiah, plus new material. This book gives a fresh look at what I wrote about the Messiah's temple found in Ezekiel 40-48.

Probably the most neglected section in the entire Bible is Ezekiel chapters 40-48. This section of the Scriptures reveals King Messiah reigning in His magnificent temple in Jerusalem. There is seldom any preaching on these Scriptures and even less teaching. The Church for the most part has ignored it. This book addresses that neglect.

Ezekiel 40-48 is really the most powerful section of Scriptures in the Old Testament to prove that King Messiah is the God of Israel. It conclusively proves that the New Covenant is now in force, and it contains enigmas which cannot be answered under the law of Moses. The only answers to these problems can be found in the New Covenant. When one understands the teachings of Ezekiel 40-48 about King Messiah's magnificent temple, it becomes a dream come true for an apologist of the Lord Jesus.

This book is the direct result of Judaism's antimissionaries challenging me over the gospel of Jesus of Nazareth.

The antimissionaries claim since there are sacrifices in the Messiah's temple, then the death of Jesus on the cross could not be the final sacrifice for sin as stated in Hebrews 10:12.

Literally, thousands of hours of research and study have gone into this book. The information in this book has been tested by email and verbal debates with rabbis and Judaism's antimissionaries. The majority of the teachings in this book have all come from the fires of debate, and like the first book of this series this one comes from direct interaction through debate with people who have made it their life goal to discredit the gospel of the Lord Jesus.

Through the law of King Messiah's temple, the New Covenant can be proven. The Messiah being the God of Israel can be proven, and huge issues are raised for which the law of Moses has no answers.

An example of an enigma which cannot be resolved in the Old Testament is that the Ark of the Covenant has been removed from any future use in the Messiah's temple. During the reign of King Messiah, there will be no more Ark of the Covenant. This is easily understood in the New Testament because the Ark is replaced by the throne of David, upon which is seated Jesus of Nazareth, King Messiah.

It is my hope that the material in this book will strengthen the faith of all who read it. This information will be used as a witnessing tool to win the lost to the Savior, and it will be a challenge to all who do not believe that Jesus of Nazareth is the King Messiah of Israel.

The Messiah's magnificent temple proves without a doubt that Jesus of Nazareth is Israel's King Messiah. One day in the future, the Lord Jesus will be seated on His throne in His temple in full glory as both King of Israel and High Priest. He alone can sit on the throne of David. Why has the Church neglected this teaching for so many years? The time has come that Ezekiel 40-48 no longer be neglected, but used as a powerful teaching tool and an even more powerful evangelical tool.

Part One

King Messiah's Temple and The Throne of David

CHAPTER ONE

The Coming
of King Messiah

"And he said unto me, Son of man, the place
of my throne, and the place of the soles of
my feet, where I will dwell in the midst of
the children of Israel for ever, and my holy
name, shall the house of Israel no more
defile..." Ezekiel 43:7

One of the most awe inspiring teachings in the Bible is
the coming of King Messiah, Jesus of Nazareth, to
establish His everlasting Kingdom on earth. He will be
coming in awesome power and glory. The coming of King
Messiah will be supernatural, and the entire earth will be
shaken at His presence. He is coming with the "clouds of
heaven," which is a term for the believers in heaven with
Him. In the New Testament, the "clouds of heaven" is also
referred to as the "armies of heaven."

Revelation 19:14 "And the armies which were
in heaven followed him upon white horses,

clothed in fine linen, white and clean."

When the Lord Jesus returns at His second coming, He will have with Him a huge host of believers. This is going to be an incredible event. The prophet Daniel wrote about His coming. The Scriptures follow:

> Daniel 7:13 "I saw in the night visions, and, behold, one like the Son of man came with the clouds of heaven, and came to the Ancient of days, and they brought him near before him.
> (14) And there was given him dominion, and glory, and a kingdom, that all people, nations, and languages, should serve him: his dominion is an everlasting dominion, which shall not pass away, and his kingdom that which shall not be destroyed."

Everyone living at this time will see the awesome coming of the Son of Man to establish His Kingdom. The coming of King Messiah to establish His Kingdom is also referred to as the second coming of Jesus of Nazareth. His coming is going to affect every living being on the earth. What an awesome day this will be, when the Lord returns in awesome glory to establish His everlasting kingdom on earth.

> Revelation 1:7 "Behold, he cometh with clouds; and every eye shall see him, and they also which pierced him: and all kindreds of the earth shall wail because of him."

When King Messiah returns, it will be to Israel and the city of Jerusalem. Jerusalem will be the future spiritual, political and economic center of the earth. The Bible shows that the coming of King Messiah will be triggered by the armies of the world gathered in the Middle East to destroy Israel and capture Jerusalem. There will be a worldwide upheaval at this time and incredible wars that kill one-third of mankind. The Lord Jesus will return directly to Jerusalem and defend His covenant people Israel from the nations which have gathered to destroy them. He will instantly destroy the armies that have gathered together to try and annihilate Israel. The Bible gives a vivid description of what is going to happen to these armies and how they are going to be annihilated. These Scriptures follow:

> Zechariah 14:2 "For I will gather all nations against Jerusalem to battle; and the city shall be taken, and the houses rifled, and the women ravished; and half of the city shall go forth into captivity, and the residue of the people shall not be cut off from the city.
> (3) Then shall the LORD go forth, and fight against those nations, as when he fought in the day of battle. (4) And his feet shall stand in that day upon the Mount of Olives, which is before Jerusalem on the east...
> (12) And this shall be the plague wherewith the LORD will smite all the people that have fought against Jerusalem; Their flesh shall consume away while they stand upon their feet, and their eyes shall consume away in their holes, and their tongue shall consume away in their mouth."

At the time of His coming, there will be a tremendous geographical upheaval in the nations, but especially in Israel. There will be massive earthquakes that will shake the entire earth and flatten the cities of the world. The Mount of

Olives, which is just east of Mount Zion, will split in two and create a huge valley.

Through all this geographical upheaval, a huge area around Jerusalem will be made a plain and raised up like a high mountain. A river will flow from the temple in Jerusalem to both the Mediterranean Sea to the west and the Dead Sea to the east.

The setting for the coming of King Messiah will be tremendous geographical changes to Israel and Jerusalem. The Bible calls this time period the Day of the Lord. The prophet Zechariah shows that the Day of the Lord has four phases.

The first phase is when all the nations are gathering together to try and take Jerusalem; the second is the coming of the Lord Jesus to destroy these nations; the third is the building of the temple; and the final phase is when the Lord Jesus rules on the throne of David from Jerusalem.

Some of the key Scriptures regarding the Day of the Lord's phases and the geographic changes to Jerusalem follow:

The Day of the Lord and the nations gathered to battle against Jerusalem. First Phase:

> Zechariah 14:1 "Behold, the day of the LORD cometh, and thy spoil shall be divided in the midst of thee. (2) For I will gather all nations against Jerusalem to battle; and the city shall be taken, and the houses rifled, and the women ravished; and half of the city shall go forth into captivity, and the residue of the people shall not be cut off from the city."

The massive earthquake. Second Phase:

> Zechariah 14:4 "And his feet shall stand in that day upon the Mount of Olives, which is

before Jerusalem on the east, and the Mount of Olives shall cleave in the midst thereof toward the east and toward the west, and there shall be a very great valley; and half of the mountain shall remove toward the north, and half of it toward the south.

(5) And ye shall flee to the valley of the mountains; for the valley of the mountains shall reach unto Azal: yea, ye shall flee, like as ye fled from before the earthquake in the days of Uzziah king of Judah: and the LORD my God shall come, and all the saints with thee."

The plain around Jerusalem will rise like a high mountain. Third Phase:

Zechariah 14:10 "All the land shall be turned as a plain from Geba to Rimmon south of Jerusalem: and it shall be lifted up, and inhabited in her place, from Benjamin's gate unto the place of the first gate, unto the corner gate, and from the tower of Hananeel unto the king's winepresses.

(11) And men shall dwell in it, and there shall be no more utter destruction; but Jerusalem shall be safely inhabited."

King Messiah ruling from the throne of David. Fourth Phase:

Isaiah 2:3 "And many people shall go and say, Come ye, and let us go up to the mountain of the LORD, to the house of the God of Jacob; and he will teach us of his ways, and we will walk in his paths: for out of Zion shall go forth the law, and the word of the

> LORD from Jerusalem."
> Ezekiel 43:7 "And he said unto me, Son of man, the place of my throne, and the place of the soles of my feet, where I will dwell in the midst of the children of Israel for ever..."

After King Messiah returns and destroys the armies of the nations, He will build a magnificent temple in Jerusalem. The temple will be built on the high plain that now encompasses Jerusalem. He will sit on His throne in this temple as King over all the nations. This temple on Mount Zion will be the spiritual and political center of the entire earth.

Ezekiel identifies this future massive plain that Jerusalem is on as a very high mountain. The Scriptures to show that the temple will be built on this high plain that is Jerusalem follow:

> Ezekiel 40:2 "In the visions of God brought he me into the land of Israel, and set me upon a very high mountain, by which was as the frame of a city on the south."
> Ezekiel 43:12 "This is the law of the house; Upon the top of the mountain the whole limit thereof round about shall be most holy. Behold, this is the law of the house."

CHAPTER TWO

The Branch of David Builds the Temple

Zechariah 6:11 "Then take silver and gold, and make crowns, and set them upon the head of Joshua the son of Josedech, the high priest;

(12) And speak unto him, saying, Thus speaketh the LORD of hosts, saying, Behold the man whose name is The BRANCH; and he shall grow up out of his place, and he shall build the temple of the LORD:

(13) Even he shall build the temple of the LORD; and he shall bear the glory, and shall sit and rule upon his throne; and he shall be a priest upon his throne: and the counsel of peace shall be between them both."

The above section of the Bible is absolutely critical to understanding the role of King Messiah in the temple. These Scriptures need a very close examination to grasp fully what God is saying through the prophet Zechariah. The key to understanding these Scriptures is the Branch and the information developed about Him. When the message is understood, the key chapters of Ezekiel 40-48 about the temple become very clear.

The prophets Zechariah and Haggai wrote immediately after the Babylonian captivity. When the Jews returned, they found the city and temple destroyed. They began to rebuild the temple under the direction of Zerubbabel who was the governor and Joshua the high priest. Haggai wrote to encourage the building of the temple. Zechariah then uses the building of the second temple to show what is going to take place with the building of the Messiah's temple.

When Zechariah wrote these Scriptures, the second temple was already under construction for about five months. The prophet Haggai spoke the word of the LORD in the second year of the rule of king Darius on the first of the sixth month. The order went out from the LORD to build the temple. Zerubbabel and Joshua responded by starting the construction, Haggai 1:1,2,12. When Zechariah wrote chapter six the temple had been under construction for five months, Zechariah 1:7.

Zechariah, at the direction of the LORD, makes crowns of gold and silver for a king. He then places the crowns on the head of Joshua the high priest. God's high priest never wore the crown of a king, instead he wore a head covering called a mitre. Today, a mitre would be called a turban. Zechariah then addresses the high priest with the crowns of a king on his head as, "Behold the man whose name is the BRANCH." The high priest was used as an object lesson to reveal the BRANCH.

> Zechariah 6:12 "And speak unto him, saying, Thus speaketh the LORD of hosts, saying, Behold the man whose name is The BRANCH; and he shall grow up out of his place, and he shall build the temple of the LORD:"

Zechariah used the building of the second temple and the high priest as an object lesson. The temple was already under construction, but the prophet was talking about a future temple. This person, the Branch, is going to build this temple of the LORD. He is going to sit and rule upon His throne. When He is sitting as King, He will also function as the High Priest. The combination of Him being a King and High Priest is going to bring peace.

> Zechariah 6:13 "Even he shall build the temple of the LORD; and he shall bear the glory, and shall sit and rule upon his throne; and he shall be a priest upon his throne: and the counsel of peace shall be between them both."

The Branch then becomes a very key figure. The prophet goes on to say that the Branch shall build the temple. In fact, the prophet emphasizes this by twice stating that the Branch is going to build the temple. He says this in verse 12 and again in verse 13.

With the object lesson of the high priest wearing crowns, it is clear that the Branch is being addressed as two office holders. He is both a king and priest in one person. The identity of the Branch is very important.

The Branch cannot be Zerubbabel. The kingdom was taken away from Judah at this time, and the Jews were under the authority of the Persians. Darius was king and Zerubbabel was only a mere governor under Darius. Zerubbabel never ruled as a king on the throne of David, and he never bore the glory. Zerubbabel never functioned as a priest and Joshua never functioned as a king.

It is impossible for this section of Scripture to be Zerubbabel or Joshua or a combination of them both. This is a prophecy about one individual who is identified as the

Branch. The throne mentioned is the throne of David. The Branch, being King Messiah, will sit on the throne of David. It is very important to realize the throne that the Branch will sit on is the throne of David. There will be only one throne when the Branch is ruling.

The prophet used Joshua as both king and high priest to show what the Branch was going to do in the future. He was going to build the final temple of the LORD. This is the temple which will be built by King Messiah and described in Ezekiel chapters 40-48.

The Bible uses the name, the BRANCH, as an identifier of King Messiah. The Branch is a term to signify King Messiah who is a direct descendant of King David. The prophets Isaiah, Jeremiah, and Zechariah all refer to King Messiah as the Branch. It is the Branch of David, King Messiah, who will build the magnificent temple of Ezekiel 40-48 from which He shall rule the nations.

Thus the Bible very clearly teaches that the Branch is going to build His temple. He is going to hold the office of both King and High Priest. As He sits as both King and Priest, He is going to bear the glory, and there will be world-wide peace under Him. This is the everlasting kingdom that was promised to David.

The Hebrew word for Branch is *tsemach*, Strong's Exhaustive Concordance number 6780. It literally means a sprout and gives the picture of something growing. The Branch then, is King Messiah, who is a descendant of David. The Hebrew word tsemach is only found nine times in the Bible and five times it is translated Branch.

Each time the word is translated Branch, it gives an additional picture of the Messiah. The first use is by Isaiah who describes the Branch as beautiful and glorious. Isaiah also shows the time when the Branch will reign. The time frame will be during King Messiah's reign on earth when Israel will be called holy. This verse follows:

> Isaiah 4:2 "In that day shall the branch of the
> LORD be beautiful and glorious, and the fruit
> of the earth shall be excellent and comely for
> them that are escaped of Israel. (3) And it
> shall come to pass, that he that is left in Zion,
> and he that remaineth in Jerusalem, shall be
> called holy, even every one that is written
> among the living in Jerusalem:"

Jeremiah gives very important Scriptures about King
Messiah being the Branch of David. He states that God is
going to raise up a righteous Branch to David. The Branch
will be King over all the earth. He will execute judgment
and justice in earth. Israel will dwell safely. This is the same
time frame when King Messiah is ruling over the earth.
King Messiah and the Branch of David are one and the
same. The Branch will be called, THE LORD OUR RIGH-
TEOUSNESS. Jeremiah without any doubt shows that the
Branch is King Messiah.

> Jeremiah 23:5 "Behold, the days come, saith
> the LORD, that I will raise unto David a
> **righteous Branch**, and a King shall reign
> and prosper, and shall execute judgment and
> justice in the earth. (6) In his days Judah shall
> be saved, and Israel shall dwell safely: and
> this is his name whereby he shall be called,
> THE LORD OUR RIGHTEOUSNESS."

Jeremiah uses the Hebrew word *tsemach* for a second time
to identify King Messiah as the Branch of David. In Chapter
33, he again refers to King Messiah as the Branch of righteousness from David. The Branch is going to execute judgment and righteousness in the land and there will be peace
and safety. When the Branch is ruling, Jerusalem will be

referred to as the LORD our righteousness. This is because of the presence of the Branch in the city.

> Jeremiah 33:15 "In those days, and at that time, will I cause the Branch of righteousness to grow up unto David; and he shall execute judgment and righteousness in the land. (16) In those days shall Judah be saved, and Jerusalem shall dwell safely: and this is the name wherewith she shall be called, The LORD our righteousness."

The next reference to the Branch is found in Zechariah. The prophet refers to the Branch as God's Servant and thus it becomes a very important reference. King Messiah, the Branch and God's Servant are all one person.

Zechariah shows that when God brings forth His Servant, that iniquity is going to be removed from the people in one day. There is then a direct connection between God's Servant, the Branch, and the cleansing from sin. The Scriptures to show this follow:

> Zechariah 3:8 "Hear now, O Joshua the high priest, thou, and thy fellows that sit before thee: for they are men wondered at: for, behold, I will bring forth my servant **the BRANCH.**
>
> (9) For behold the stone that I have laid before Joshua; upon one stone shall be seven eyes: behold, I will engrave the graving thereof, saith the LORD of hosts, and I will remove the iniquity of that land in one day."

The last reference in the Bible to the Branch is found in Zechariah 6, showing the Messiah to be both King and

Priest. From the previous verses, it is clear that the Branch is the King Messiah, and He is going to rule in righteousness over the entire earth. He will bring peace and safety not only to Israel, but to all the nations of the world. Zechariah clearly states that King Messiah is going to build the temple, and He is going to be both King and High Priest. He is going to sit on His throne, the throne of David and bear the glory.

There is no doubt that Zechariah 6:11-13 is an object lesson to what the Branch is going to do and what He is going to be. He will sit on the throne as both King and High Priest, and He will bear the glory. The Scriptures to show this follow:

> Zechariah 6:12 "And speak unto him, saying, Thus speaketh the LORD of hosts, saying, Behold the man whose name is The BRANCH; and he shall grow up out of his place, and he shall build the temple of the LORD:
> (13) Even he shall build the temple of the LORD; and he shall bear the glory, and shall sit and rule upon his throne; and he shall be a priest upon his throne: and the counsel of peace shall be between them both."

When studying the Scriptures about the temple in Ezekiel chapters 40-48, it is critical to remember that the Messiah will build this temple and sit on the throne of David as both King and High Priest. This is the foundation for understanding the rest of the Scriptures about the temple. Without this understanding, the Messiah's temple can be very confusing. With King Messiah sitting on the throne of David in the temple, everything else about the temple fits perfectly together.

CHAPTER THREE

Messiah as Both King and Priest

"Then take silver and gold, and make crowns, and set them upon the head of Joshua the son of Josedech, the high priest; (12) And speak unto him, saying, Thus speaketh the LORD of hosts, saying, Behold the man whose name is The BRANCH; and he shall grow up out of his place, and he shall build the temple of the LORD:"
Zechariah 6:11,12

King Messiah will build the temple, bear the glory, and sit upon the throne as both King and Priest. Only God's servant, the Branch, can sit on the throne in the temple as both King and High Priest.

Under the law of Moses the king and high priest could never be united under one person. Both being a king or high priest depended on genealogy The kings were from the tribe of Judah and the line of David while the high priests were from the tribe of Levi and the line of Aaron. Thus, it was impossible for the same person to be both king and priest. The two separate lines are shown in the Scriptures which follow:

> Jeremiah 33:17,18 "For thus saith the LORD;
> David shall never want a man to sit upon the
> throne of the house of Israel; Neither shall the
> priests the Levites want a man before me to
> offer burnt offerings, and to kindle meat
> offerings, and to do sacrifice continually."

The penalty was death for anyone but the high priest to enter into the most holy place of the temple and minister. It was impossible for any king of Israel to enter into the holy place and minister as a priest. In the entire course of the history of the kings of Israel and Judah in the Bible, there is not one report of the king entering into the temple and functioning as a high priest.

Neither king David nor Solomon ever went into the most holy place of the temple. For anyone other than the descendants of Aaron entering, it meant certain death. This is shown in the following verses:

> Numbers 4:15 "And when Aaron and his sons
> have made an end of covering the sanctuary,
> and all the vessels of the sanctuary, as the
> camp is to set forward; after that, the sons of
> Kohath shall come to bear it: **but they shall
> not touch any holy thing, lest they die**...
>
> (19) "But thus do unto them, that they may
> live, **and not die**, when they approach unto
> the most holy things: Aaron and his sons
> shall go in, and appoint them every one to his
> service and to his burden: (20) But they shall
> not go in to see when the holy things are
> covered, **lest they die**."

Thus, under the law, it was impossible for one person to be both the king of Israel and the high priest at the same time.

The throne of David will be in the holy place of the temple. For King Messiah to sit on the throne in the holy of holies, He also has to be a priest. He cannot be just a priest, but He has to be the high priest to enter into the most holy place.

This shows that God's servant, the Branch, is going to sit on His throne in the temple not under the law of Moses, but He will be King and Priest under the New Covenant. God's servant, the Messiah, will be both King and Priest by the decree of Almighty God and not because of human genealogy. The office of king and priest will merge in Him because of the decree made by the holy God of Israel.

By God's decree the Branch is declared to be the Son of God and thus King Messiah. Notice the connection between the King of Israel and the Son of God. By God's decree, He is declared to be the High Priest, not after the law of Moses and the genealogy of Aaron. The Scriptures to show both of these decrees follow:

Messiah is King because He is declared to be the begotten Son of God:

> Psalm 2:6 "Yet have I set my king upon my holy hill of Zion. (7) I will declare the decree: the LORD hath said unto me, Thou art my Son; this day have I begotten thee.
>
> (8) Ask of me, and I shall give thee the heathen for thine inheritance, and the uttermost parts of the earth for thy possession. (9) Thou shalt break them with a rod of iron; thou shalt dash them in pieces like a potter's vessel."

Messiah is Priest because God declares it:

> Psalm 110:4 "The LORD hath sworn, and will not repent, Thou art a priest for ever after the order of Melchizedek."

Melchizedek, a Type of the Messiah

Before the law was given to Moses, the Bible records that Melchizedek came to Abraham and blessed him. Melchizedek was both a king and priest. He was the king of Salem and at the same time a priest of the most high God. Psalm 110 states that by a decree of God, the Messiah is going to be the Priest of the most high God after the manner of Melchizedek. According to Psalm 2, the Messiah is King, so like Melchizedek, He is going to be both King and Priest. The passage to show this follows:

> Genesis 14:18 "And Melchizedek king of Salem brought forth bread and wine: and he was the priest of the most high God. (19) And he blessed him, and said, Blessed be Abram of the most high God, possessor of heaven and earth:"

A priest is one who intercedes or mediates on behalf of man before God. This is seen in Leviticus 16 during the Day of Atonement, when the high priest went into the very presence of God in the temple. He went in with the blood of a sacrificed animal that died and atoned for the sins of Israel. So, likewise, God's Messiah will be a Priest before God.

The Messiah would go once into the holy place in heaven to make the final atonement for sin. This would be accomplished with His own blood for the final redemption for sin.

> Hebrews 9:12 "Neither by the blood of goats and calves, but by his own blood he entered in once into the holy place, having obtained eternal redemption for us."

The previous temples and priesthood on earth were simply a type of the final one King Messiah would bring under the New Covenant. The New Testament is right in line with Psalm 2:7 and 110:4 as it refers to the Messiah as both the High Priest and King. Jesus of Nazareth was both King and Priest, by the decree of God. The New Testament Scriptures follow:

> Hebrews 5:5 "So also Christ glorified not himself to be made an high priest; but he that said unto him, Thou art my Son, to day have I begotten thee.
> (6) As he saith also in another place, Thou art a priest for ever after the order of Melchisedec."

In summary, the Messiah is going to build the temple from which He is going to rule over the nations forever. The kingdom of King Messiah will not be for a limited period of time, but it will be forever. He will reign on into eternity when heaven and earth are merged. The temple will be built in Jerusalem after the battle of Armageddon and after the geography of Israel is radically changed.

According to Psalm 2:6,7, King Messiah is going to sit on the throne of David in His magnificent temple as the Son of God. He can enter into the holy place in the temple and sit on the throne because He is God's eternal High Priest after the order of Melchizedek. With this background, let us examine Ezekiel 40-48 which gives great detail about the temple and King Messiah.

King Messiah's Temple

> "And the man said unto me, Son of man, behold with thine eyes, and hear with thine

> ears, and set thine heart upon all that I shall show thee; for to the intent that I might show them unto thee art thou brought hither: declare all that thou seest to the house of Israel." Ezekiel 40:4

Ezekiel chapters 40 through 48 describe King Messiah's temple in Jerusalem. These chapters describe in great detail the magnificent temple that will be built by the Messiah, the Branch of David. These Scriptures detail how the Messiah will be sitting on His throne, ruling the entire world. This will be the time when Israel, under the glory of the Messiah, will be exalted among the nations of the earth. The prophet Ezekiel refers to the temple as God's house, and the terms house and temple are interchangeable.

The most striking aspect of God's house is that it is full of the glory of God. It is full of God's glory because the God of Israel is in it! The prophet Ezekiel writes how he watched the God of Israel in His glory enter into the temple by the outer East Gate. The glory of God was so brilliant that Ezekiel compared it to the sun. He heard the voice of the LORD speak from the house.

Ezekiel was so overwhelmed by the glory of God and the power of His voice that he fell upon his face. Twice the prophet fell down because he was in the awesome presence of God's majestic glory.

Ezekiel was very clear and there was no mistaking that the God of Israel was literally in His house. This is King Messiah's temple which will be built by Him, yet the God of Israel in His glory is there! He enters into the temple through the East Gate which is then sealed! The Scriptures showing God in His glory in the temple follow:

The holy God of Israel in His glory is in the temple:
Ezekiel 43:2 "And, behold, **the glory of the**

God of Israel came from the way of the east: and his voice was like a noise of many waters: and the earth shined with his glory. (3) ...I fell upon my face. (4) And the **glory of the LORD came into the house** by the way of the gate whose prospect is toward the east. (5) So the spirit took me up, and brought me into the inner court; and, behold, **the glory of the LORD filled the house.** (7) And he said unto me, Son of man, **the place of my throne**, and the place of the soles of my feet, where I will dwell in the midst of the children of Israel for ever, and my holy name, shall the house of Israel no more defile,"

The God of Israel literally entered into the temple by the East Gate:

Ezekiel 44:1 "Then he brought me back the way of the gate of the outward sanctuary which looketh toward the east; and it was shut. (2) Then said the LORD unto me; This gate shall be shut, it shall not be opened, and no man shall enter in by it; because **the LORD, the God of Israel,** hath entered in by it, therefore it shall be shut. (4) Then brought he me the way of the north gate before the house: and I looked, and, behold, **the glory of the LORD filled the house of the LORD:** and I fell upon my face."

The very last Scripture of Ezekiel shows that, when King Messiah reigns, Jerusalem will be given an additional name.

Because the God of Israel is dwelling in Jerusalem, the city is going to be also called, JEHOVAH shammah, or the LORD is there. The prophet Ezekiel makes it very clear that the God of Israel will be dwelling in His house in Jerusalem.

The name of Jerusalem will be actually changed to reflect the presence of God in the city! The New Testament closes the same way with a view of the New Jerusalem and God dwelling amongst His people. These Scriptures follow:

> Ezekiel 48:35 "...and the name of the city from that day shall be, The LORD is there."
>
> Revelation 21:3 "And I heard a great voice out of heaven saying, Behold, the tabernacle of God is with men, and he will dwell with them, and they shall be his people, and God himself shall be with them, and be their God."

The Messiah, King of Kings

The Scriptures clearly teach that the Messiah will be King over all the earth. According to Zechariah 6:12-13, the Branch shall sit and rule upon His throne after the temple is built. Not only is this King identified as the Messiah, He is the LORD Himself.

In the LORD's house, it becomes clear that the God of Israel and the Messiah of Israel are the same. King Messiah and the LORD God of Israel are both sitting on the same throne in the temple. It is the throne of David that Zechariah so carefully wrote the Branch would sit upon.

The Son of God ruling the nations as King Messiah in Psalm 2:6-9 is the God of Israel sitting on His throne in the temple, Ezekiel 43:7. Comparisons of Daniel 7:13,14; Psalm 2:6-9; Zechariah 6:12,13; and Ezekiel 43:4-7 show that King Messiah is the God of Israel. These comparisons follow:

King Messiah coming in glory to establish His kingdom:
> Daniel 7:13 "I saw in the night visions, and, behold, one like the Son of man came with the clouds of heaven, and came to the Ancient of days, and they brought him near before him.
> (14) And there was given him dominion, and glory, and a kingdom, that all people, nations, and languages, should serve him: his dominion is an everlasting dominion, which shall not pass away, and his kingdom that which shall not be destroyed."

King Messiah is the Son of God ruling the nations with a rod of iron:
> Psalm 2:6 "Yet have I set my king upon my holy hill of Zion. (7) I will declare the decree: the LORD hath said unto me, Thou art my Son; this day have I begotten thee.
> (8) Ask of me, and I shall give thee the heathen for thine inheritance, and the uttermost parts of the earth for thy possession. (9) Thou shalt break them with a rod of iron; thou shalt dash them in pieces like a potter's vessel."

King Messiah to build the temple and sit on the throne of David as King:
> Zechariah 6:12-13 "Behold the man whose name is The BRANCH; and he shall grow up out of his place, and he shall build the temple of the LORD:
> (13) Even he shall build the temple of the LORD; and he shall bear the glory, **and shall sit and rule upon his throne**; and he shall

be a priest upon his throne: and the counsel
of peace shall be between them both."

The God of Israel is sitting on the Messiah's throne, the
throne of David:
> Ezekiel 43:4 "And the glory of the LORD
> came into the house by the way of the gate
> whose prospect is toward the east...
>
> (7) And he said unto me, Son of man, **the
> place of my throne**, and the place of the
> soles of my feet, where I will dwell in the
> midst of the children of Israel for ever, and
> my holy name, shall the house of Israel no
> more defile..."

The fundamental doctrine of Christianity is the holy God of
Israel is King Messiah. This is proven in the Old Testament
by the Scriptures listed above. Zechariah 6:11-13 reveals
that the Branch, the Messiah of Israel, will build His temple
and sit on the throne of David and bear the glory. Ezekiel
43:7 shows the God of Israel in His glory is sitting on the
throne, reserved for the Messiah, the throne of David.

CHAPTER FOUR

Israel's King Messiah the Son of God

> 2 Samuel 7:14 "I will be his father, and he shall be my son. If he commit iniquity, I will chasten him with the rod of men, and with the stripes of the children of men:"

In addition to King Messiah being the God of Israel, He is further identified as the Son of God. This is the second foundation of Christianity and both can be clearly seen by King Messiah seated on the throne of David.

God's everlasting covenant with King David established the first direct connection with Israel's King Messiah as being the son of God. This happened in approximately 1000 BC. Solomon sat on the throne of David as the King of Israel. Because Solomon was the King of Israel, God declared Himself to be his Father and Solomon His son. He was the first king of Israel under this covenant and a type of the last king who would be King Messiah, the begotten Son of God.

Thus we see in Scripture that God's everlasting covenant

with David did establish the first connection to show King Messiah as the Son of God. David's son Solomon sat on the throne as God's chosen son as well as Israel's king. From this position, we can then see that Solomon becomes a type or picture of King Messiah. He is the first king who leads directly to King Messiah. However, the Son of God will sit forever on the throne of David.

God's Everlasting Covenant with David

The Bible records the covenant God made with King David regarding his throne. The Scriptures reveal two very important characteristics of this covenant. First, God establishes an everlasting kingdom, and secondly God introduces a Father-son relationship with the king so that Solomon would reign as God's chosen son. This covenant is found in 2 Samuel 7:13-16:

> 2 Samuel 7:13 "He shall build an house for my name, and I will stablish the throne of his kingdom **for ever**. (14) **I will be his father, and he shall be my son**. If he commit iniquity, I will chasten him with the rod of men, and with the stripes of the children of men:
> (15) But my mercy shall not depart away from him, as I took it from Saul, whom I put away before thee. (16) And thine house and thy kingdom shall be established **for ever** before thee: thy throne shall be established **for ever.**"

In these verses, God makes it very clear that David's throne and the kingdom will be forever and not simply limited to David and Solomon. Both David and Solomon died about

3000 years ago, so this promise obviously could not be made exclusively to them, but God proclaimed that King Messiah would be of David's seed. There is no doubt that the Messiah's reign and His throne and His kingdom would be forever. The Scriptures supporting 2 Samuel 7:13-15 give very important additional information about King Solomon and his reign. King David reinforces that Solomon will follow him as king. He then shows that Solomon is not to reign simply as the king of Israel, but he is to sit on the throne of the kingdom of the LORD over Israel. Thus Solomon represents the God of Israel on earth as the king over Israel.

Thus according to Scripture, God was to be Solomon's Father, and Solomon would be God's chosen son. Solomon sat on **the throne of the Lord** over Israel as the son of God:

> 1 Chronicles 28:4 "Howbeit the LORD God of Israel chose me before all the house of my father to be king over Israel for ever: for he hath chosen Judah to be the ruler; and of the house of Judah, the house of my father; and among the sons of my father he liked me to make me king over all Israel:"
>
> (5) "And of all my sons, (for the LORD hath given me many sons,) he hath chosen Solomon my son to sit upon the throne of **the kingdom of the LORD** over Israel. (6) And he said unto me, Solomon thy son, he shall build my house and my courts: **for I have chosen him to be my son, and I will be his father."**

With the foundation that Solomon reigned over Israel as the son of God, we can now compare this with King Messiah's reign. King Messiah will have dominion over the entire earth and not only Israel. All the nations will come under His authority, and He will rule them with a "rod of iron."

While Solomon was the chosen son of God, King Messiah who rules over all the nations will be the begotten Son of God. King David was Solomon's father, but the God of Israel is King Messiah's Father. He will rule the nations with God's decree that He was begotten of God and not man:

> Psalm 2:6 "Yet have I set my king upon my holy hill of Zion. (7) I will declare the decree: the LORD hath said unto me, Thou art my Son; this day have I begotten thee."
>
> (8) "Ask of me, and I shall give thee the heathen for thine inheritance, and the uttermost parts of the earth for thy possession. (9) Thou shalt break them with a rod of iron; thou shalt dash them in pieces like a potter's vessel."

God's promise to David was eternal. It was not limited to David or Solomon, but it reached to the eternal kingdom of King Messiah. The very authority of God's word and character bridges this covenant because it originates from His holiness.

God promised to bring His begotten Son into the world to rule the nations as King Messiah. And the Scriptures show that the begotten Son of God would reign forever as King Messiah based on the everlasting covenant God made with King David:

> Psalm 132:11 "The LORD hath sworn in truth unto David; he will not turn from it; Of the fruit of thy body will I set upon thy throne."

> Psalm 89:34 "My covenant will I not break, nor alter the thing that is gone out of my lips. (35) Once have I sworn by my holiness that I will not lie unto David. (36) His seed shall endure for ever, and his throne as the sun before me."

The New Testament
And
The Son of God

When the Lord Jesus was arrested and tried, the High Priest interrogated Him about His identity. The Lord did not respond to the questioning until the High Priest asked Him in the name of the living God if He was the Christ, the Son of God. Jesus replied by combining Psalm 110:1 and Daniel 7:13,14 for His answer. Thus He claimed to be King Messiah, the Son of God according to the Hebrew Scriptures.

The High Priest was well aware that King Messiah would be the Son of God. He understood the everlasting covenant with David. And he knew the promise that 2 Samuel 7:13-15, 1 Chronicles 28:4-6 and Psalm 2:6-9 provides regarding King Messiah as the Son of God. When Jesus responded that He was the Son of God, the High Priest rent, tore, his clothes and said the Lord Jesus should die because He had committed blasphemy.

Jesus claimed to be the Son of God. This claim was in perfect agreement with the Hebrew Scriptures. The Jews expected King Messiah to be the Son of God, but many rejected that Jesus of Nazareth was this promised Son.

> Matthew 26:63 "But Jesus held his peace. And the high priest answered and said unto him, I adjure thee by the living God, that

thou tell us whether thou be **the Christ, the Son of God**.

(64) Jesus saith unto him, Thou hast said: nevertheless I say unto you, Hereafter shall ye see the Son of man sitting on the right hand of power, and coming in the clouds of heaven.

(65) Then the high priest rent his clothes, saying, He hath spoken blasphemy; what further need have we of witnesses? behold, now ye have heard his blasphemy."

When the Lord ascended to heaven, God proclaimed Him to be King Messiah, the begotten Son of God. He is the Holy One, David and the prophets wrote would rule the nations forever.

Acts 13:32 "And we declare unto you glad tidings, how that the promise which was made unto the fathers, (33) God hath fulfilled the same unto us their children, in that he hath raised up Jesus again; as it is also written in the second psalm, Thou art my Son, this day have I begotten thee."

In heaven, the Lord Jesus is seated on the throne of God. All of heaven acknowledges that He is the Root of David. He reigns in heaven as the Son of David, the Son of God. Henceforth, God's throne in heaven is directly connected to the throne of David. At the Lord's second coming, His throne will be transferred to earth where He will reign as the Branch of David on the throne of David.

Revelation 5:5 "And one of the elders saith unto me, Weep not: behold, the Lion of the tribe of Juda, the **Root of David**, hath prevailed to open the book, and to loose the seven seals thereof.

(6) And I beheld, and, lo, in the midst of **the throne** and of the four beasts, and in the midst of the elders, stood a Lamb as it had been slain, having seven horns and seven eyes, which are the seven Spirits of God sent forth into all the earth."

When King Messiah returns, He will come in His awesome glory. His throne will be established on earth in Jerusalem on Mount Zion. He will reign as King over all the earth as the begotten Son of God, sitting on the throne of the LORD according to God's everlasting covenant with David. At this time, Israel will be exalted, and He will rule all the nations of the earth from the throne of David.

Matthew 25:31 "When the Son of man shall come in his glory, and all the holy angels with him, then shall he sit upon the throne of his glory: (32) And before him shall be gathered all nations: and he shall separate them one from another, as a shepherd divideth his sheep from the goats:"

Thus He will establish the everlasting covenant of peace with Israel and restore them to the land given to Jacob. He will build the sanctuary of the LORD on Mount Zion and rule over all the nations, not just Israel. King Messiah will sit on the throne of David and rule the nations with a rod of iron as the begotten Son of God. This is the claim of the New Testament about Jesus of Nazareth. This New Testament doctrine rests on a solid foundation in the Old Testament.

God's Magnificent Throne

Ezekiel does not describe God's throne in the most holy place of the temple. However, in other Scriptures the prophet gives a vivid description of what the throne will look like in the temple. Ezekiel used the precious stone sapphire, brilliant blue, to describe the color over the throne. The entire throne had an amber or bronze color. Ezekiel described the throne in awesome colors with tremendous brightness and the appearance of fire all around it. The entire throne was surrounded with brightness that looked like a rainbow.

Ezekiel witnessed the God of Israel sitting on His throne. God was in the appearance of a man. God gave the appearance of being totally on fire. Ezekiel said that the brightness of the throne was the glory of the Lord. He fell upon his face before this glory.

Ezekiel's description of God sitting on His throne follows:

> Ezekiel 1:26 "And above the firmament that was over their heads was the likeness of a throne, as the appearance of a sapphire stone: and upon the likeness of the throne was the likeness as the appearance of a man above upon it.
>
> (27) And I saw as the colour of amber, as the appearance of fire round about within it, from the appearance of his loins even upward, and from the appearance of his loins even downward, I saw as it were the appearance of fire, and it had brightness round about.
>
> (28) As the appearance of the bow that is in the cloud in the day of rain, so was the appearance of the brightness round about.

> This was the appearance of the likeness of
> the glory of the LORD. And when I saw it, I
> fell upon my face, and I heard a voice of one
> that spake."

Notice when Ezekiel saw the God of Israel sitting on His throne, He was in the form of a man. God was in a form that Ezekiel could recognize as a man. When God is sitting on His throne in His house, it will again be in the form of a man. God will be sitting on the throne of David in the person of the Lord Jesus, King Messiah.

Ezekiel saw the same glory in the temple coming from the Messiah's throne. The awesome throne, which Ezekiel so vividly described, is the very throne that the Lord Jesus will sit and rule upon. What an incredible sight this will be, the glory of God emanating from His magnificent throne from His house in Jerusalem.

The Scriptures to show that the glory of God's throne is the same glory that came from the temple follow:

> Ezekiel 1:28 "As the appearance of the
> bow that is in the cloud in the day of rain, so
> was the appearance of the brightness round
> about. This was the appearance of the like-
> ness of the **glory of the LORD**. And when I
> saw it, I fell upon my face, and I heard a
> voice of one that spake."
>
> Ezekiel 44:4 "Then brought he me the way
> of the north gate before the house: and I
> looked, and, behold, **the glory of the LORD**
> filled the house of the LORD: and I fell upon
> my face."

In the New Testament, the Scriptures show that at the second coming of the Lord Jesus, He will sit on the throne of His glory, the throne of David. This is the throne that Ezekiel so vividly described. The throne will be located in the most holy place of King Messiah's awesome temple on top of Mount Zion.

> Matthew 25:31 "When the Son of man shall come in his glory, and all the holy angels with him, then shall he sit upon the throne of his glory: (32) And before him shall be gathered all nations: and he shall separate them one from another, as a shepherd divideth his sheep from the goats"

In the Day of the Lord, when King Messiah is reigning, there will be only one King over all the earth. He will be ruling from His house, and will sit and rule upon His throne in Zion. The Bible never speaks of two kings reigning but only one. Jesus of Nazareth, King Messiah, ruling over the nations and the LORD God of Israel ruling as King are the same person.

All the nations of the earth will come to Jerusalem and worship King Messiah, the LORD of hosts. The Scriptures to show there will be only one king of Israel over all the earth follow:

> Ezekiel 37:22 "And I will make them one nation in the land upon the mountains of Israel; and one king shall be king to them all: and they shall be no more two nations, neither shall they be divided into two kingdoms any more at all:"
>
> Zechariah 14:9 "And the LORD shall be king over all the earth: in that day shall there be one LORD, and his name one."
>
> (16) "And it shall come to pass, that every

one that is left of all the nations which came against Jerusalem shall even go up from year to year to worship the King, the LORD of hosts, and to keep the feast of tabernacles.

(17) And it shall be, that whoso will not come up of all the families of the earth unto Jerusalem to worship the King, the LORD of hosts, even upon them shall be no rain."

The Messiah, the LORD God of Israel, will sit upon His throne in Zion. He will rule the nations and be in the midst of the children of Israel forever. There is only one throne mentioned in Ezekiel 40-48. In God's house there is only one throne, and it is located in the most holy place. The God of Israel in His glory is sitting on this throne. There are not two or three thrones but just one. This throne is reserved for the Messiah, and the God of Israel as King Messiah will sit on it in His majestic glory.

Thus He will rule the nations from this throne. What a glorious day this is going to be when the Lord Jesus, King Messiah, is ruling the nations from the midst of His people Israel!

God Desires to Dwell Among His People

The Bible shows that God desires to dwell among His people. God desires fellowship with man so greatly, that He was willing to become a man in the person of King Messiah. The psalms show that it is the desire of the God of Israel to dwell in Zion for His habitation. The prophet Zephaniah shows that God's joy of dwelling in Jerusalem is so great that He will sing when He is in the midst of His people. Zephaniah calls God's presence in His house a "rest in his love."

The prophet Zechariah shows that there will be singing and rejoicing because the God of Israel will be dwelling in the midst of Zion. What a mental picture this gives. The people are singing and rejoicing because God is dwelling in His house, and God, so overwhelmed with joy, that He is singing with His people. What a day this will be when the God of Israel is singing for joy from His house on Mount Zion! The Scriptures to show this follow:

Psalm 132:13 "For the LORD hath chosen Zion; he hath desired it for his habitation. (14) This is my rest for ever: here will I dwell; for I have desired it."

Zephaniah 3:14 "Sing, O daughter of Zion; shout, O Israel; be glad and rejoice with all the heart, O daughter of Jerusalem. (15) The LORD hath taken away thy judgments, he hath cast out thine enemy: the king of Israel, even the LORD, is in the midst of thee: thou shalt not see evil any more.

(16) In that day it shall be said to Jerusalem, Fear thou not: and to Zion, Let not thine hands be slack. (17) The LORD thy God in the midst of thee is mighty; he will save, he will rejoice over thee with joy; he will rest in his love, he will joy over thee with singing."

Zechariah 2:10 "Sing and rejoice, O daughter of Zion: for, lo, I come, and I will dwell in the midst of thee, saith the LORD."

CHAPTER FIVE

The Law of the Temple

"This is the law of the house; Upon the top
of the mountain the whole limit thereof
round about shall be most holy. Behold, this
is the law of the house." Ezekiel 43:12

In chapters 40-42, great detail is given to the dimensions
of the temple, the walls surrounding it and the entrance
gates to it. The exact dimensions are given with precise
measurements. The temple complex will be a huge square
with the outside walls measuring approximately 900 feet on
each side. Parts of this temple complex are 100 to 120 feet
high. Even the designs on the paneling of the inside of the
temple are given. The temple will be engraved with palm
trees and cherubim.

Great detail is also given to describe the altar of sacrifice
and the feasts which will be celebrated during this time.
God tells Ezekiel to show Israel the form of the house and
everything connected with it. Ezekiel was to write what he
saw as the LAW, and this is called the law of the house. In
three chapters, Ezekiel was commanded by God to write
what he witnessed. What Ezekiel wrote will be the law

under King Messiah. This is the law of the temple, and it will be observed under King Messiah. If Ezekiel did not mention an item or a festival, then it was not there.

Thus what Ezekiel witnessed he wrote as he was directed by God Himself. King Messiah is holy, and the temple structure and laws all reflect God's holiness. At that time, Jerusalem will be called God's holy mountain.

The verses to show that everything involving the temple will be holy follow:

> Ezekiel 43:12 "This is the law of the house; Upon the top of the mountain the whole limit thereof round about shall be most holy. Behold, this is the law of the house."
>
> Isaiah 66:20 "And they shall bring all your brethren for an offering unto the LORD out of all nations upon horses, and in chariots, and in litters, and upon mules, and upon swift beasts, to my holy mountain Jerusalem...
>
> Obadiah 1:17 "But upon mount Zion shall be deliverance, and there shall be holiness; and the house of Jacob shall possess their possessions."
>
> Zechariah 8:3 "Thus saith the LORD; I am returned unto Zion, and will dwell in the midst of Jerusalem: and Jerusalem shall be called a city of truth; and the mountain of the LORD of hosts the holy mountain."

This law will supersede the law of Moses. It is vastly different than the ordinances under Moses. The Messiah's house will be vastly different than previous temples or the tabernacle in the wilderness. All this is because King Messiah will reign under the New Covenant and not the covenant at Sinai.

Three times God told Ezekiel to carefully observe all that he witnessed and heard. What Ezekiel wrote from this experience was the law of the house. The Scriptures showing the law of the temple follow:

> Ezekiel 40:4 "And the man said unto me, Son of man, behold with thine eyes, and hear with thine ears, and set thine heart upon all that I shall show thee; for to the intent that I might show them unto thee art thou brought hither: declare all that thou seest to the house of Israel."
>
> Ezekiel 43:11 "...show them the form of the house, and the fashion thereof, and the goings out thereof, and the comings in thereof, and all the forms thereof, and all the ordinances thereof, and all the forms thereof, and all the laws thereof: and write it in their sight, that they may keep the whole form thereof, and all the ordinances thereof, and do them." (12) "This is the **law of the house**; Upon the top of the mountain the whole limit thereof round about shall be most holy. Behold, this is the **law of the house**."
>
> Ezekiel 44:5 "And the LORD said unto me, Son of man, mark well, and behold with thine eyes, and hear with thine ears all that I say unto thee concerning all the ordinances of the house of the LORD, and all the laws thereof; and mark well the entering in of the house, with every going forth of the sanctuary."

King Messiah will Teach This Law From the temple

When the Lord Jesus returns and establishes His kingdom, all the nations of the earth will come to Jerusalem to worship Him and be taught the law of God. All the people will flow into Jerusalem to be taught. According to Ezekiel, the law that will be taught will be the law of the temple. The entire structure of the temple, plus the feasts and ordinances all have spiritual meaning and this will be the law that is taught. This law teaches God's holiness.

The law of the temple will have a direct relationship to the New Covenant. Under the New Covenant, the law of the temple will become known in the earth as the waters cover the sea. It is King Messiah who will teach this law and explain all the meanings of His magnificent temple and the ordinances of it.

He will teach how all the ordinances show His work on the cross for the redemption of man from sin. The temple and everything associated with it will be an object lesson. All this will show the holiness of God. All the nations will flow into Jerusalem to be taught by King Messiah the law of the house and not the law of Moses:

> Isaiah 2:2 "And it shall come to pass in the last days, that the mountain of the Lord's house shall be established in the top of the mountains, and shall be exalted above the hills; and all nations shall flow unto it.
>
> (3) And many people shall go and say, Come ye, and let us go up to the mountain of the LORD, to the house of the God of Jacob; and he will teach us of his ways, and we will walk in his paths: for out of Zion shall go forth the law, and the word of the LORD from Jerusalem.

The full knowledge of the LORD will be under the New Covenant and not the covenant of the law under Moses. The New Covenant is internal with God's word written on the heart. This is far different than the law of Moses:

> Jeremiah 31:31 "Behold, the days come, saith the LORD, that I will make a new covenant with the house of Israel, and with the house of Judah: (32) Not according to the covenant that I made with their fathers in the day that I took them by the hand to bring them out of the land of Egypt...
>
> (33) But this shall be the covenant that I will make with the house of Israel; After those days, saith the LORD, I will put my law in their inward parts, and write it in their hearts; and will be their God, and they shall be my people.
>
> (34) And they shall teach no more every man his neighbour, and every man his brother, saying, Know the LORD: for they shall all know me, from the least of them unto the greatest of them, saith the LORD: for I will forgive their iniquity, and I will remember their sin no more."

What is Absent from the Messiah's House is Very Important

Ezekiel was told to write about the temple and the fashion or the equipment of it. He wrote exactly what he witnessed in the temple and what it contained. Inside the huge magnificent temple building was the throne of King Messiah and a small table. Outside the temple, he saw a large altar for sacrifice. The only pieces of equipment were a small table before the throne and the altar.

In Ezekiel 43:11,12, notice how, in great detail, the prophet is told to write all that he sees. He is to write about the design of the temple, the fashions, all the forms and ordinances, plus all the comings and goings that are associated with the temple. The prophet writes inclusively, nothing was left out.

> Ezekiel 43:11 "...show them the form of the house, and the fashion thereof, and the goings out thereof, and the comings in thereof, and all the forms thereof, and all the ordinances thereof, and all the forms thereof, and all the laws thereof: and write it in their sight, that they may keep the whole form thereof, and all the ordinances thereof, and do them.
>
> (12) This is the law of the house; Upon the top of the mountain the whole limit thereof round about shall be most holy. Behold, this is the law of the house."

What Ezekiel described was called the law of the temple. If Ezekiel did not report it, then the temple item or the feast under the law of Moses was not there. These items or feasts will not be present under the reign of the Lord Jesus. Note one of the radical differences: Ezekiel's temple will have the throne of David which was absent from all the previous temples.

The fact that Ezekiel failed to record any additional items in the temple is of great importance. The Tabernacle in the Wilderness and Solomon's temple both had key equipment which will be absent from King Messiah's house.

A list of the major missing items follows: Menorah,

Table of Shewbread, Altar of incense, Veil that hid the most holy place, Laver of Brass, Ark of the Covenant and the office of Aaronic high priest. The law of the temple is radically different from the law of Moses and these two cannot be reconciled.

A comparison of the previous temples with King Messiah's shows that the items missing are not needed because they are replaced by the presence of King Messiah. These were all types or representations of King Messiah and His ministry. With the physical presence of King Messiah on the throne of David, there will no longer be any need for these items, including the high priest.

Before examining these items, it is important to understand the layout of the temples. The first temple was called the tabernacle in the wilderness. It will be referred to as the tabernacle. God gave Moses the design and fixtures in it.

See pages 92-93 with diagrams showing the contrast between the Tabernacle under the law of Moses and the Temple under the law of the House.

The two previous temples built in Jerusalem followed this design. They all had a main rectangular edifice divided in two sections; the holy place and the most holy place. King Messiah's temple will retain the general physical layout of the holy place and the most holy place together in one building.

Under the law of Moses, the holy place contained the menorah, table of Shewbread and the altar of incense. The most holy place was separated by a veil and had the Ark of the Covenant in it. The high priest could only go into the most holy place once a year on the Day of Atonement. Just outside the entrance to the temple were the altar of sacrifice and the laver of brass.

An examination of each of these missing items that are

types shows how the Lord Jesus fulfilled them. Let's examine each item to show how Jesus of Nazareth, King Messiah fulfilled them:

Ark of the Covenant

The most important item in the tabernacle was the Ark. The Ark was box shaped and about four feet by two feet by two feet in size. It was made of wood overlaid with gold. The Ark was located in the most holy place behind the veil. This veil separated the most holy place from the rest of the temple. Placed in the Ark were the stone tablets which the 10 Commandments were written on, a pot of manna and Aaron's rod that budded. The Ark had a solid gold cover which also had two gold cherubim with their wings spread. Cherubim are angelic beings that are always near the throne of God.

The top of the cover was called the Mercy Seat. Once every year the high priest would sprinkle blood on the Mercy Seat to atone for sin. God's presence literally hovered just over the Mercy Seat and between the two cherubim.

> Exodus 25:22 "And there I will meet with thee, and I will commune with thee from above the mercy seat, from between the two cherubims which are upon the Ark of the Testimony..."

The prophet Jeremiah ties together the Ark and the throne of God. Jeremiah said the day would come when the Ark would no longer be remembered or even thought of because Jerusalem would become the throne of God. This would happen under the reign of King Messiah when all the nations would come to Jerusalem to worship and man's heart would be free of evil. These Scriptures follow:

Jeremiah 3:16 "And it shall come to pass, when ye be multiplied and increased in the land, in those days, saith the LORD, they shall say no more, The ark of the covenant of the LORD: neither shall it come to mind: neither shall they remember it; neither shall they visit it; neither shall that be done any more. (17) At that time they shall call Jerusalem the throne of the LORD; and all the nations shall be gathered unto it, to the name of the LORD, to Jerusalem: neither shall they walk any more after the imagination of their evil heart."

When King Messiah is reigning there will be no Ark. The Ark is not mentioned under the law of the temple. It has been replaced by the throne of God just as Jeremiah 3;16,17 stated it would be. In the holy of holies, the throne of David will replace the Ark. When the Lord Jesus is reigning, it will be from this throne in the most holy place of the temple.

Just as Jeremiah stated, there will be no more Ark. The Ark will not be mentioned, nor will it be thought of, nor will it be remembered. Why would anyone think of the Ark, when the God of Israel in His glory is sitting on the throne of David!

The Ark was the type or shadow but the throne of David the reality. This is a very important concept which Jeremiah 3:16,17 is showing. The Ark was only a type of God seated on His throne. When God is actually seated on the throne, there is no need for the Ark. This concept of a piece of the temple equipment being a type is very important when examining the furnishings of the LORD's house.

The following Scriptures clearly show the Throne of David has replaced the Ark:

Ezekiel 43:5 "So the spirit took me up, and brought me into the inner court; and, behold, the glory of the LORD filled the house. (6) And I heard him speaking unto me out of the house... (7) And he said unto me, Son of man, **the place of my throne**, and the place of the soles of my feet, where I will dwell in the midst of the children of Israel for ever, and my holy name, shall the house of Israel no more defile,..."

Jeremiah 3:16 "And it shall come to pass, when ye be multiplied and increased in the land, in those days, saith the LORD, they shall say no more, The ark of the covenant of the LORD: neither shall it come to mind: neither shall they remember it; neither shall they visit it; neither shall that be done any more.

(17) At that time they shall call Jerusalem the throne of the LORD; and all the nations shall be gathered unto it, to the name of the LORD, to Jerusalem: neither shall they walk any more after the imagination of their evil heart."

God's presence hovered over the Ark, but His fullness in His glory will be on the throne in His house. The Ark contained the 10 Commandments, the pot of manna, and Aaron's rod that budded. The Commandments represent the word of God; the manna God's supernatural life from heaven; and Aaron's rod represented resurrection from the dead. All three being housed in the Ark point directly to King Messiah. When He is seated on His throne, He is the word of God. He is our supernatural life from heaven while He is also the resurrection and the life.

King Messiah is the word of God in the flesh:
> John 1:1 "In the beginning was the Word, and the Word was with God, and the Word was God. (14) And the Word was made flesh, and dwelt among us, (and we beheld his glory, the glory as of the only begotten of the Father,) full of grace and truth."

King Messiah is manna from heaven:
> John 6:49 "Your fathers did eat manna in the wilderness, and are dead. (50) This is the bread which cometh down from heaven, that a man may eat thereof, and not die.
>
> (51) I am the living bread which came down from heaven: if any man eat of this bread, he shall live for ever: and the bread that I will give is my flesh, which I will give for the life of the world."

King Messiah is the resurrection and the life:
> John 11:25 "Jesus said unto her, I am the resurrection, and the life: he that believeth in me, though he were dead, yet shall he live: (26) And whosoever liveth and believeth in me shall never die. Believest thou this?"

Veil of Separation

> Exodus 26:33 "And thou shalt hang up the veil under the taches, that thou mayest bring in thither within the veil the ark of the testimony: and the veil shall divide unto you between the holy place and the most holy."

In the previous temples and the tabernacle, between the holy place in the temple and the most holy place was a veil. No one could look directly into the holy place where the Ark of the Covenant was located. The high priest would go through the veil into the most holy place once a year to atone for the sin of the people.

Now through the death and resurrection of Jesus of Nazareth, man is no longer separated from the holy God of Israel because of sin. There is absolutely no need for a veil in King Messiah's house to separate Him from His people.

> Matthew 27:50 "Jesus, when he had cried again with a loud voice, yielded up the ghost. (51) And, behold, the veil of the temple was rent in twain from the top to the bottom; and the earth did quake, and the rocks rent;"
>
> Hebrews 10:19 "Having therefore, brethren, boldness to enter into the holiest by the blood of Jesus, (20) By a new and living way, which he hath consecrated for us, through the veil, that is to say, his flesh;"

Menorah or Candlestick

> Exodus 25:31 "And thou shalt make a candlestick of pure gold: of beaten work shall the candlestick be made...(37) And thou shalt make the seven lamps thereof: and they shall light the lamps thereof, that they may give light over against it."

In the holy place of the tabernacle and the previous temples was the pure, golden menorah to give light. The literal glory of the Messiah is going to light His house. There will be no need for a menorah. Of far greater importance than lighting the temple is King Messiah being the light of the world. In the presence of King Messiah, there will be no spiritual darkness. The menorah only pointed to the Messiah being the light of the world.

The following Scriptures show this:

> Isaiah 2:4 "And he shall judge among the nations, and shall rebuke many people: and they shall beat their swords into plowshares, and their spears into pruninghooks: nation shall not lift up sword against nation, neither shall they learn war any more. (5) O house of Jacob, come ye, and let us walk in the light of the LORD."
>
> John 1:4 "In him was life; and the life was the light of men."
>
> John 8:12 "Then spake Jesus again unto them, saying, I am the light of the world: he that followeth me shall not walk in darkness, but shall have the light of life."

Table of Shewbread

> "Exodus 25:23 "Thou shalt also make a table of shittim wood: two cubits shall be the length thereof, and a cubit the breadth thereof, and a cubit and a half the height thereof. (30) And thou shalt set upon the table Shewbread before me alway."

In the holy place was a golden table with 12 loaves of unleavened bread placed on it. Bread is the staple of physical life. King Messiah is the sustainer of both physical and spiritual life. With the presence of King Messiah, there is no need for a Table of Shewbread. He is the bread of life.

> John 6:35 "And Jesus said unto them, I am the bread of life: he that cometh to me shall never hunger; and he that believeth on me shall never thirst."

Altar of Incense

> Leviticus 16:12 "And he shall take a censer full of burning coals of fire from off the altar before the LORD, and his hands full of sweet incense beaten small, and bring it within the veil: (13) And he shall put the incense upon the fire before the LORD, that the cloud of the incense may cover the mercy seat that is upon the testimony, that he die not"

This altar was in the holy place just before the veil that separated the holy place from the most holy place. It was used on the Day of Atonement as part of the ceremony to atone for sin. With the presence of King Messiah and being under the New Covenant, it is no longer needed.

> Hebrews 9:11 "But Christ being come an high priest of good things to come, by a greater and more perfect tabernacle, not made with hands, that is to say, not of this building;
> (12) Neither by the blood of goats and calves, but by his own blood he entered in once into the holy place, having obtained eternal redemption for us."

Laver of Brass

> Exodus 30:18 "Thou shalt also make a laver of brass, and his foot also of brass, to wash withal: and thou shalt put it between the tabernacle of the congregation and the altar, and thou shalt put water therein."

Between the altar of sacrifice and the entrance to the tabernacle was the laver of brass. The laver was a round and deep, bath like object. The priests would cleanse themselves in it before entering into the tabernacle. The washing of the body before ministering before the holy God of Israel was a picture of being spiritually clean.

Through the words of King Messiah, there is no longer a need for the laver. Sinners become clean through His word and shed blood. The Scriptures to show this follow:

> Zechariah 13:1 "In that day there shall be a fountain opened to the house of David and to the inhabitants of Jerusalem for sin and for uncleanness."
>
> John 15:3 "Now ye are clean through the word which I have spoken unto you."
>
> Ephesians 5:25 "Husbands, love your wives, even as Christ also loved the church, and gave himself for it; (26) That he might sanctify and cleanse it with the washing of water by the word"
>
> Hebrews 10:21 "And having an high priest over the house of God; (22) Let us draw near with a true heart in full assurance of faith, having our hearts sprinkled from an evil conscience, and our bodies washed with pure water."

Israel will be sprinkled clean at the second coming of the Lord Jesus. The sprinkling to cleanse Israel at the coming of the Messiah is very similar to the washing of water in the laver before coming into the presence of the LORD in the tabernacle.

The sprinkling of water is a picture of being made clean by the work of the Holy Spirit within a person's heart. It is cleansing of the heart from sin that makes a person clean before the holy God of Israel. Washing with water in the laver is a picture of being cleansed by the word and Spirit of God under King Messiah.

The idea of the laver of brass will be fulfilled at the second coming of King Messiah when Israel will be made clean. There will be no need for the laver in King Messiah's house. Israel will be clean and holy before Him. The prophet Ezekiel very clearly shows how Israel is going to be cleansed. This cleansing will occur when God places a new spiritual heart in a person. The old heart of stone and sin is replaced with a heart of flesh.

> Ezekiel 36:24 "For I will take you from among the heathen, and gather you out of all countries, and will bring you into your own land. (25) Then will I sprinkle clean water upon you, and ye shall be clean: from all your filthiness, and from all your idols, will I cleanse you.
>
> (26) A new heart also will I give you, and a new spirit will I put within you: and I will take away the stony heart out of your flesh, and I will give you an heart of flesh."

Office of the High Priest

> Leviticus 16:4 "He shall put on the holy
> linen coat, and he shall have the linen
> breeches upon his flesh, and shall be girded
> with a linen girdle, and with the linen mitre
> shall he be attired: these are holy garments;
> therefore shall he wash his flesh in water,
> and so put them on."

God told Ezekiel to write what he witnessed and this would
be the law of the temple. Ezekiel wrote about the priests
ministering to the LORD. He even described their dress, but
there was no mention of the high priest. With great detail,
He mentions the priests ministering before the Lord and a
description of their garments. The priests are given instruc-
tions on how to dress when they minister before King
Messiah.

The high priest normally wore beautifully colored
garments with a breastplate and a mitre (turban) with a gold
band inscribed on the front "Holiness To The Lord." On the
Day of Atonement, he took off the beautiful garments and
wore simple white garments when he went into the holy
place. The garments the high priest wore on this day were
called holy garments. This is the type of garments the
priests will wear before King Messiah, holy garments.

Thus Ezekiel describes priests ministering before King
Messiah, but there is no mention of a high priest. The high
priest or his special garments are never mentioned under the
law of the temple. The priests ministering before the Lord are
always plural and not one can be identified as the high priest.

> Ezekiel 44:17 "And it shall come to pass,
> that when they enter in at the gates of the
> inner court, they shall be clothed with linen

garments; and no wool shall come upon them, whiles they minister in the gates of the inner court, and within. (18) They shall have linen bonnets upon their heads, and shall have linen breeches upon their loins; they shall not gird themselves with any thing that causeth sweat."

When King Messiah is reigning there is no need for an Aaronic high priest. He is the eternal high priest. His eternal priesthood replaces the Aaronic high priest system. There is no veil blocking the throne and therefore, no need for the sprinkling of blood on the mercy seat. There is no Ark, but there is a throne.

The one who shed His blood to redeem mankind is sitting on the throne; therefore, He is now the eternal High Priest. The priesthood will be under the Melchizedek high priest in the temple.

There has been a change in the priesthood from one of genealogy from Aaron, to King Messiah which is based on an oath. Because of this there also has to be a change in the law. The Melchizedek priesthood is under the New Covenant and not the law of Moses. The Scriptures to show this follow:

Hebrews 7:11 "If therefore perfection were by the Levitical priesthood, (for under it the people received the law,) what further need was there that another priest should rise after the order of Melchisedec, and not be called after the order of Aaron? (12) For the priesthood being changed, there is made of necessity a change also of the law.

(15) "And it is yet far more evident: for that after the similitude of Melchisedec there ariseth another priest, (16) Who is made, not

after the law of a carnal commandment, but after the power of an endless life."

The One Item that Remains Under the Law of the Temple: The Altar of Sacrifice

> Ezekiel 43:15 "So the altar shall be four cubits; and from the altar and upward shall be four horns."

The one item that carried over from the tabernacle is the altar of sacrifice. This altar is described in great detail along with the sacrifices that are going to be offered on it. The altar will be directly in front of the entrance to the temple. King Messiah sitting on His throne will be able to watch the ceremony on the altar. The priest offering the sacrifice will walk up the steps of the altar and face directly into the temple. He can look through and see the Messiah sitting on his throne as he is conducting the ritual.

Under the New Covenant, God will remember sin no more; therefore, the offering made on this altar will be for memorials to what King Messiah did on the cross.

> Jeremiah 31:31 "Behold, the days come, saith the LORD, that I will make a new covenant with the house of Israel, and with the house of Judah: (34)...for I will forgive their iniquity, and I will remember their sin no more."

He will teach the full spiritual meaning of the altar and the sacrifices. The nations will flow to Jerusalem to be taught the law of the temple by the Son of God sitting on His throne!

> Micah 4:2 "And many nations shall come, and say, Come, and let us go up to the mountain of the LORD, and to the house of the God of Jacob; and he will teach us of his ways, and we will walk in his paths: for the law shall go forth of Zion, and the word of the LORD from Jerusalem

King Messiah will teach how the entire tabernacle and law of the temple pointed to His coming. He will teach how everything about the temple is holy.

> Hebrews 10:10 "By the which will we are sanctified through the offering of the body of Jesus Christ once for all."

The Feasts of Israel

All items in the tabernacle pointed to King Messiah, so too, the seven feasts along with the Sabbath and new moon also point to Him. Ezekiel identifies only three feasts that are a part of the temple law. These feasts are Passover, Unleavened bread and Tabernacles. There is no mention of the other feasts which were given under the law of Moses. Those feasts are Firstfruits, Pentecost, Trumpets and the Day of Atonement. All the feasts, whether mentioned or not, point to the person and ministry of King Messiah.

At this present time, four of the feasts have been fulfilled at the first coming of King Messiah. These are: Passover, Unleavened bread, Firstfruits and Pentecost. At King Messiah's second coming the remaining three will be fulfilled. All seven of the feasts together give the complete picture of the ministry of King Messiah.

> John 5:39 "Search the Scriptures; for in them ye think ye have eternal life: and they are they which testify of me."

When King Messiah is teaching the law of the temple from Mount Zion, He will be explaining how all the feasts point to Him. He will show how the feasts all were fulfilled by His first and second coming. He will especially use the Feasts of Passover and Tabernacles as object lessons that represent Him.

> Luke 24:44 "And he said unto them, These are the words which I spake unto you, while I was yet with you, that all things must be fulfilled, which were written in the law of Moses, and in the prophets, and in the psalms, concerning me."

All the Hebrew Scriptures point to King Messiah, the Branch of David. The entire structure and ordinances of King Messiah's house will be a teaching related to Him. The law of the temple will be taught and not the law of Moses. The Lord Jesus will teach the law of the temple to the people.

> Ezekiel 43:12 "...This is the law of the house; Upon the top of the mountain the whole limit thereof round about shall be most holy. Behold, this is **the law of the house."**
> Isaiah 2:3 "And many people shall go and say, Come ye, and let us go up to the mountain of the LORD, to the house of the God of Jacob; and he will teach us of his ways, and we will walk in his paths: **for out of Zion shall go forth the law**, and the word of the LORD from Jerusalem."

The Feasts Observed Under the Law of the Temple

Ezekiel reported only three of the feasts for the law of the temple. These feasts are found in Ezekiel 45:21-24. The feasts are Passover, Unleavened bread and Tabernacles. Each one of these feasts has a direct tie to King Messiah. They point to Him and His ministry. The plan of God's salvation for mankind can be seen in these feasts which are under the law of the temple.

The first feast that God gave to Moses was Passover-Unleavened bread and the last was Tabernacles. The first and last of the feasts are the very ones to be observed under King Messiah. Passover starts with deliverance from God's judgment by the death and shed blood of the lamb placed on the door posts. Tabernacles ends with the joyous harvest. The harvest represents the multitude from the nations who now believe in Israel's King Messiah. The feasts start with the death of the lamb and end with the gathering of the nations:

> Zechariah 14:16 "And it shall come to pass, that every one that is left of all the nations which came against Jerusalem shall even go up from year to year to worship the King, the LORD of hosts, and to keep the feast of tabernacles."

A review of The Three Feasts

Passover-Unleavened Bread

> Exodus 12:13 "And the blood shall be to you for a token upon the houses where ye are: and when I see the blood, I will pass over you, and the plague shall not be upon you to

> destroy you, when I smite the land of Egypt.
> (14) And this day shall be unto you for a
> memorial; and ye shall keep it a feast to the
> LORD throughout your generations; ye shall
> keep it a feast by an ordinance for ever."

Passover and Unleavened bread go together as feasts. Passover shows how the children of Israel were protected when the judgment of death fell on Egypt. The death of a lamb and then posting the blood on the door of the home caused the death angel to pass over that residence and spare the life of the first born. Israel was protected from death because of the lamb that died in the place of the first born.

Moses instituted the Passover feast as a memorial to the deliverance of the children of Israel from Egypt. The law of King Messiah's house will observe Passover and Unleavened bread. Passover will be a tremendous object lesson for King Messiah to teach the nations. The first Passover was when the children of Israel were delivered from the judgment of the death angel on Egypt by the death and blood of the lamb.

> Exodus 12:26 "And it shall come to pass,
> when your children shall say unto you, What
> mean ye by this service (27) That ye shall
> say, It is **the sacrifice** of the LORD's
> passover, who passed over the houses of the
> children of Israel in Egypt, when he smote
> the Egyptians, and delivered our houses..."

The Feast of Passover was to be kept as a memorial down through the generations by the command of the Scriptures. The reason it was to be kept was because of the sacrifice that protected the children of Israel from the death angel. The sacrifice of the lamb and posted blood are the very heart of the Feast of Passover. God wants the focus of Passover to be on the sacrifice, death of the lamb and the shed blood for protection. The Lamb of God is now seated on the throne of David. What a teaching lesson this will be for the people. The Passover will be kept under the Law of the temple:

> Ezekiel 45:21 "In the first month, in the fourteenth day of the month, ye shall have the passover, a feast of seven days; unleavened bread shall be eaten."
> John 1:29 "The next day John seeth Jesus coming unto him, and saith, Behold the Lamb of God, which taketh away the sin of the world."

The Lord's Supper just before His crucifixion shows how Passover was a picture of His death. Through the Lord's death and shed blood, the people were delivered from the judgment for sin by King Messiah, the Lamb of God. The Lord Jesus tied together the sacrifice of the Passover lamb and unleavened bread to Himself at the Last Supper.

> 1 Corinthians 11:23 "For I have received of the Lord that which also I delivered unto you, That the Lord Jesus the same night in which he was betrayed took bread: (24) And when he had given thanks, he brake it, and said, Take, eat: this is my body, which is broken for you...."

The key to the Feast of Passover was the sacrifice of the lamb and the displaying of its shed blood. This act delivered the children of Israel from the death angel. The key to the New Covenant is the death and shed blood of King Messiah for deliverance from sin and eternal judgment.

In the law of the house, the Feast of Passover will be observed. King Messiah, the LAMB of God, will sit on His throne in His temple and watch the Passover. This is such a beautiful picture of our redemption from sin by His death and shed blood.

> 1 Corinthians 5:7 "Purge out therefore the old leaven, that ye may be a new lump, as ye are unleavened. For even Christ our passover is sacrificed for us:"
>
> 1 Peter 1:18 "Forasmuch as ye know that ye were not redeemed with corruptible things, as silver and gold, from your vain conversation received by tradition from your fathers; (19) But with the precious blood of Christ, as of a lamb without blemish and without spot:"

Leaven or yeast in the Bible is a picture of sin. Leaven is a picture of sin permeating a person's life and taking over. Unleavened is a picture of holiness. King Messiah is the bread of life. He is without sin or leaven. He is holy and without sin.

> 1 Corinthians 5:8 "Therefore let us keep the feast, not with old leaven, neither with the leaven of malice and wickedness; but with the unleavened bread of sincerity and truth."

Tabernacles

> Leviticus 23:34 "Speak unto the children of Israel, saying, The fifteenth day of this seventh month shall be the feast of tabernacles

> for seven days unto the LORD." (39) ...when
> ye have gathered in the fruit of the land, ye
> shall keep a feast unto the LORD"

This will be the last feast to be observed under the law of the Messiah's house. This feast is always observed at the end of the harvest which is around September-October. This was to be a joyous feast with the completion of the harvest. This feast was a type when King Messiah would reign and all the nations would worship before Him. This feast will be a great joy.

> Ezekiel 45:25 "In the seventh month, in the
> fifteenth day of the month, shall he do the
> like in the feast of the seven days,"

The reign of King Messiah will be just like a Feast of Tabernacles. It will be a joyous time with plenty of food. It will also be a joyous time as all the nations of the world come before King Messiah as a type of harvest. The prophet Zechariah so clearly ties together the nations coming before the Lord with the Feast of Tabernacles.

> Zechariah 14:16 "And it shall come to pass,
> that every one that is left of all the nations
> which came against Jerusalem shall even go
> up from year to year to worship the King, the
> LORD of hosts, and to keep the feast of
> tabernacles."

The bringing in of the physical harvest is a picture of the nations coming before the Lord Jesus. In the law of God's house, King Messiah will show how the Feast of Tabernacles is a picture of the great harvest of the nations that come before Him. His reign will be one continuous

Feast of Tabernacles!

The Sabbath and the Law of the Temple

> Exodus 31:15 "Six days may work be done; but in the seventh is the Sabbath of rest, holy to the LORD: whosoever doeth any work in the Sabbath day, he shall surely be put to death."

The Sabbath will be one of the main festivals under King Messiah. According to the law of the house, the Sabbath will be kept. The Sabbath is the perfect picture of the Messiah's rule. The Sabbath is a rest from work and a day to focus on God. The Sabbath rest is viewed by God as a part of holiness before Him.

> Ezekiel 44:24 "And in controversy they (priests) shall stand in judgment; and they shall judge it according to my judgments: and they shall keep my laws and my statutes in all mine assemblies; and they shall hallow my Sabbaths."

The reign of King Messiah will be as a Sabbath rest. The reign of the LORD is compared to a glorious rest. There will be great peace and blessings not only for Israel but also for the entire world at this time. Under King Messiah, all the nations shall be brought into God's rest.

> Isaiah 11:1 "And there shall come forth a rod out of the stem of Jesse, and a Branch shall grow out of his roots: (10) And in that day there shall be a root of Jesse, which

shall stand for an ensign of the people; to it shall the Gentiles seek: and his rest shall be glorious."

The entering of the children of Israel into the promised land is called entering into God's rest. Entering the promised land is a picture of resting under the authority and blessing of God.

Psalm 95:10 "Forty years long was I grieved with this generation, and said, It is a people that do err in their heart, and they have not known my ways: (11) Unto whom I sware in my wrath that they should not enter into my rest."

When the LORD is reigning from His house, the entire world is going to be brought into His rest. The Scriptures also show that God looks upon His rule from His house as His rest!

Psalm 132:13 "For the LORD hath chosen Zion; he hath desired it for his habitation. (14) This is my rest for ever: here will I dwell; for I have desired it."

God longs to dwell in His house and be amongst His people. The prophet Zephaniah shows that this will bring such joy to God that He will actually sing in joy over the people. It is very possible that during every Sabbath the voice of the LORD will be heard singing from His throne in His house! He longs to do this.

Zephaniah 3:17 "The LORD thy God in the midst of thee is mighty; he will save, he will rejoice over thee with joy; he will rest in his love, he will joy over thee with singing."

The Sabbath is a type of resting by faith in the Messiah. During the Sabbath, one ceases from work. When one believes in the Lord Jesus, he rests from his works. The Sabbath is a picture of believing in the Lord and resting from the works of the law.

> Hebrews 4:3 "For we which have believed do enter into rest, as he said, As I have sworn in my wrath, if they shall enter into my rest: although the works were finished from the foundation of the world. (4) For he spake in a certain place of the seventh day on this wise, And God did rest the seventh day from all his works."

King Messiah is the Sabbath rest. The Sabbath is now a person and not a day. This is a most important concept to grasp: that the Sabbath is not a day of the week, but it is fulfilled in the person of King Messiah. The Sabbath points to resting by faith in the Lord Jesus for salvation.

> Colossians 2:16 "Let no man therefore judge you in meat, or in drink, or in respect of an holyday, or of the new moon, or of the Sabbath days: (17) Which are a shadow of things to come; but the body is of Christ."

During His reign, the Sabbath will be a special day with the LORD. On non-Sabbath days, the people will be able to walk through the inner court and pass before the front of the house of the Lord.

Those that enter through the North gate will pass before the entrance of the house and perhaps get a glimpse of the LORD on His throne as they exit through the South gate. Those that enter from the South gate will do the same and then exit through the North gate. There will be two lines of people passing before the entrance of the temple on non-Sabbath days.

On the Sabbath day, the Eastern gate of the inner court is opened. The Eastern gate of the outer court is permanently closed. It is closed on every day except the Sabbath. People will be allowed to enter into the inner court through the Eastern gate and congregate there. This means they will be able to look directly through the front door of the temple, which faces east, and then into the most holy place where the Lord Jesus is seated on His throne in His glory. What a special day this is going to be! The Scriptures to show this follow:

> Ezekiel 46:1 "Thus saith the Lord GOD; The gate of the inner court that looketh toward the east shall be shut the six working days; but on the Sabbath it shall be opened, and in the day of the new moon it shall be opened.
> (3) Likewise the people of the land shall worship at the door of this gate before the LORD in the Sabbaths and in the new moons."

King Messiah reigning from His house is going to be a Sabbath rest for both the Jew and the Gentile. There will be peace between God and man. Sin, as it is now, will be unknown during this time. Holiness will be the order. There will be no wars among the nations. There will be an abundant supply of food for everyone. Even nature will be changed as a child will be able to put his hand in a viper's den with no danger and the lion will lie down with the lamb.

The Four Missing Feasts of Israel

The feasts that are not mentioned all have significant importance in showing the ministry of King Messiah. The feasts that are not mentioned are: Firstfruits, Pentecost, Trumpets and the Day of Atonement. Let's examine these feasts and see how they fit the ministry of King Messiah.

Feast of Firstfruits

> Leviticus 23:10 "Speak unto the children of Israel, and say unto them, When ye be come into the land which I give unto you, and shall reap the harvest thereof, then ye shall bring a sheaf of the firstfruits of your harvest unto the priest: (11) And he shall wave the sheaf before the LORD, to be accepted for you: on the morrow after the Sabbath the priest shall wave it."

This feast was celebrated the day after the Sabbath following Passover. It was to dedicate the first of the barley harvest. The feasts of Pentecost and Tabernacles would also involve harvests. These three harvest feasts would all be a picture of the ministry of King Messiah. Firstfruits directly follows the slaying of the lamb on Passover. It is a picture of the Messiah's resurrection after the Passover. He is the first to be resurrected from the dead and the other harvest feasts show there will be multitudes following Him. These multitudes following Him in resurrection are the members of His church.

> 1 Corinthians 15:20 "But now is Christ risen from the dead, and become the firstfruits of them that slept. (23) But every man in his

own order: Christ the firstfruits; afterward they that are Christ's at his coming."

With the presence of King Messiah on His throne, there will be no need for this feast. Ezekiel did not report it; therefore, it is not a law of the temple. The Scripture showing the Feast of Firstfruits follows:

> Colossians 1:18 "And he is the head of the body, the church: who is the beginning, the firstborn from the dead; that in all things he might have the preeminence."

Feast of Weeks or Pentecost

> Deuteronomy 16:9 "Seven weeks shalt thou number unto thee: begin to number the seven weeks from such time as thou beginnest to put the sickle to the corn. (10) And thou shalt keep the feast of weeks unto the LORD thy God..."

The Feast of Pentecost follows Firstfruits. It follows 50 days after the Passover Sabbath. This feast is to dedicate the first-fruits of the wheat harvest. It is a foreshadow of the outpouring of the Holy Spirit on the Day of Pentecost. Jesus of Nazareth rose from the dead on the Feast of Firstfruits and the Holy Spirit was poured out 50 days later on Pentecost to bring in the harvest of the church.

Thus the bringing in of the harvest at Pentecost was a foreshadow of the harvest that would begin under the first coming of King Messiah. The harvest of Pentecost has continued to this day. The Scriptures to show this follow:

> Acts 2:1 "And when the day of Pentecost was fully come, they were all with one accord in one place. (2) And suddenly there came a sound from heaven as of a rushing mighty wind, and it filled all the house where they were sitting.
> (41) "Then they that gladly received his word were baptized: and the same day there were added unto them about three thousand souls."

Feast of Trumpets

> Leviticus 23:24 "Speak unto the children of Israel, saying, In the seventh month, in the first day of the month, shall ye have a Sabbath, a memorial of blowing of trumpets, an holy convocation."

The trumpet is used in Scripture to announce the coming presence of God. When the LORD came down to Mount Sinai to give the law, His coming was preceded by an incredible trumpet blast. The seventh month of the Hebrew calendar starts with the feast of Trumpets and the blast of the shofar. The Day of Atonement and then Tabernacles follow this feast. The Feast of Trumpets warns of the coming judgment and the reign of the Messiah during the period of the Feast of Tabernacles (Zechariah 14:16).

> Exodus 19:16 "And it came to pass on the third day in the morning, that there were thunders and lightnings, and a thick cloud upon the mount, and the voice of the trumpet exceeding loud; so that all the people that

> was in the camp trembled.
> (19) And when the voice of the trumpet
> sounded long, and waxed louder and louder,
> Moses spake, and God answered him by a
> voice."

The blowing of trumpets will also herald the coming of King Messiah. The reign of King Messiah will be announced by the blowing of trumpets just as God's presence was announced at Mount Sinai. This feast will have been fulfilled at the second coming of the Lord Jesus when His coming is announced with an awesome blowing of the trumpet.

With the presence of King Messiah seated on His throne in His house, there will be no need for the Feast of Trumpets. The King has arrived and is in the midst of His people.

> Matthew 24:30 "And then shall appear the
> sign of the Son of man in heaven: and then
> shall all the tribes of the earth mourn, and
> they shall see the Son of man coming in the
> clouds of heaven with power and great glory.
> (31) And he shall send his angels with a
> great sound of a trumpet..."

Day of Atonement

> Leviticus 23:27 "Also on the tenth day of this
> seventh month there shall be a day of atone-
> ment: it shall be an holy convocation unto
> you; and ye shall afflict your souls, and offer
> an offering made by fire unto the LORD."

Ezekiel recorded how King Messiah's house will be cleansed. According to the law of the temple, on the first day of the first month (March/April), a bullock will be sacrificed for sin and its blood placed on the outside of the temple on the posts, the four corners of the altar and the gates to the inner court. This procedure will also be done on the seventh day of the month for all simple errors and acts of foolishness. This is not for willful sin against the LORD.

> Ezekiel 45:18 "...In the first month, in the first day of the month, thou shalt take a young bullock without blemish, and cleanse the sanctuary: (19} And the priest shall take of the blood of the sin offering, and put it upon the posts of the house, and upon the four corners of the settle of the altar, and upon the posts of the gate of the inner court.
> (20) And so thou shalt do the seventh day of the month for every one that erreth, and for him that is simple: so shall ye reconcile the house."

These actions together will reconcile the temple. The blood being placed on the outside of the temple and the inner gate of the court, plus repeating this procedure seven days later for sin, will cleanse and reconcile the temple for the errors of the people and for the person that acts simple.

This is very important to realize that under the law of the temple, the reconciliation is for mistakes and not willful sin against the LORD. The law of the temple is for him that "erreth" and for him that is "simple." There is no reconciliation for willful sin and rebellion against God under the law of the temple. This will be shown shortly.

Comparing the law of the temple with the law of Moses shows a tremendous difference in how the temple is cleansed. The tabernacle was cleansed on the Day of Atonement by a radically different ritual. The cleansing of the house under the law of the temple shows that the Day of

Atonement has ceased.

King Messiah sitting on His throne has replaced the Day of Atonement. It is the shed blood of the Lord Jesus that first cleansed the temple in heaven and then the one on earth. This was a permanent cleansing.

> Hebrew 9:23 "It was therefore necessary that the patterns of things in the heavens should be purified with these; but the heavenly things themselves with better sacrifices than these. (24) For Christ is not entered into the holy places made with hands, which are the figures of the true; but into heaven itself, now to appear in the presence of God for us:

The Day of Atonement takes place on the tenth day of the seventh month (September/October). On the Day of Atonement, the tabernacle was cleansed by the high priest bringing blood inside the veil into the most holy place. The high priest would sprinkle the blood on the top of the Ark of the Covenant. No blood would be sprinkled on the outside of the tabernacle nor on any entrance to it.

The altar of incense and the Ark were both very important on this day. The high priest took incense from this altar and filled the room with a cloud. The blood of a goat and bullock sprinkled on the Ark inside the most holy place cleansed the tabernacle of sin and transgression. The Scriptures to show this follow:

The feast is observed during the seventh month on the tenth day. Under King Messiah the cleansing will be on the first day of the first month.

The Law of Moses:
Leviticus 23:27 "Also on the tenth day of this

seventh month there shall be a day of atonement: it shall be an holy convocation unto you; and ye shall afflict your souls, and offer an offering made by fire unto the LORD."

The Law of the Temple:

Ezekiel 45:18 "Thus saith the Lord GOD; In the first month, in the first day of the month, thou shalt take a young bullock without blemish, and cleanse the sanctuary:"

Both the incense and altar were needed on this day. There is no Altar of Incense in the Messiah's house.

Leviticus 16:12 "And he shall take a censer full of burning coals of fire from off the altar before the LORD, and his hands full of sweet incense beaten small, and bring it within the veil:"

Only the high priest could perform this ritual. There is no Aaronic high priest under the law of the temple.

Leviticus 16:2 "And the LORD said unto Moses, Speak unto Aaron thy brother, that he come not at all times into the holy place within the veil before the mercy seat, which is upon the ark; that he die not: for I will appear in the cloud upon the mercy seat."

The blood of a goat and bullock sprinkled inside the most holy place atoned/reconciled the tabernacle. Under the law of the temple there is no goat involved and the blood is placed on the outside of the temple and not brought into the inside. The Scriptures showing the irreconcilable differences between the law of Moses and the law of King

Messiah's House follow:

The law of Moses:

> Leviticus 16:15 "Then shall he kill the goat of the sin offering, that is for the people, and bring his blood within the veil, and do with that blood as he did with the blood of the bullock, and sprinkle it upon the mercy seat, and before the mercy seat:
>
> (16) And he shall make an atonement for the holy place, because of the uncleanness of the children of Israel, and because of their transgressions in all their sins: and so shall he do for the tabernacle of the congregation, that remaineth among them in the midst of their uncleanness."

The law of King Messiah's House:

> Ezekiel 45:18 "Thus saith the Lord GOD; In the first month, in the first day of the month, thou shalt take a young bullock without blemish, and cleanse the sanctuary: (19) And the priest shall take of the blood of the sin offering, and put it upon the posts of the house, and upon the four corners of the settle of the altar, and upon the posts of the gate of the inner court.
>
> (20) And so thou shalt do the seventh day of the month for every one that erreth, and for him that is simple: so shall ye reconcile the house."

The following diagram shows the location where the blood is applied during the law of King Messiah's House.

King Messiah's House
Location of the Blood Applied

Ezekiel 45:19 And the priest shall take of the blood of the sin offering, and put it upon the posts of the house, and upon the four corners of the settle of the altar, and upon the posts of the gate of the inner court.

Under the law of Moses, all the iniquities, sins and transgressions of the people were atoned by sprinkling blood on the mercy seat and confessing all sin over the scapegoat by the high priest. Under the law of the temple, only errors of the people are reconciled. There is no mention under the law of the temple of being cleansed from iniquity.

The method for reconciliation will be placing blood on the outside of the temple and not on the mercy seat in the most holy place. There will be no Ark under the law of the temple so how can the Day of Atonement be performed without the Ark?

At the end of Yom Kippur, the nation was clean before the LORD as all the iniquities, transgressions and the death and shed blood of the bullock and the goats atoned for sins of the people. All the ceremonies of Yom Kippur ended in the nation being clean before the holy God of Israel.

> Leviticus 16:21 "And Aaron shall lay both his hands upon the head of the live goat, and confess over him all the iniquities of the children of Israel, and all their transgressions in all their sins, putting them upon the head of the goat, and shall send him away by the hand of a fit man into the wilderness: (22) And the goat shall bear upon him all their iniquities…"

There is no indication under the law of the temple of Israel being made holy, righteous or clean after the rituals. The blood being placed on the outside of the temple will be a testimony to the shed blood of King Messiah seated on His throne in the most holy place. Israel will be clean and holy after King Messiah purges them of their sin and uncleanness. The Scriptures to show this follow:

Israel was clean under the law of Moses by the rituals of Yom Kippur:

> Leviticus 16:30 "For on that day shall the priest make an atonement for you, to cleanse you, that ye may be clean from all your sins before the LORD."

Israel will be holy when King Messiah purges them of their sin:

> Isaiah 4:2 "In that day shall the branch of the LORD be beautiful and glorious, and the fruit of the earth shall be excellent and comely for them that are escaped of Israel. (3) And it shall come to pass, that he that is left in Zion, and he that remaineth in Jerusalem, shall be called holy, even every one that is written among the living in Jerusalem:

(4) When the Lord shall have washed away the filth of the daughters of Zion, and shall have purged the blood of Jerusalem from the midst thereof by the spirit of judgment, and by the spirit of burning."

The law of the temple will be radically different from the law of Moses. The change is so radical only the New Covenant and King Messiah sitting on His throne can explain it. The placing of the blood on the outside of the temple shows that the Day of Atonement will no longer be observed.

Under the law of the temple, there will be no Aaronic high priest; no altar of incense, no menorah and no table of shew bread. There will be no veil separating the most holy place and no Ark of the Covenant. Even the day of cleansing the temple is radically different. It was moved from the seventh month-tenth day to the first month-first day. The Day of Atonement cannot be observed under the law of the temple.

King Messiah seated on His throne has replaced the Ark of the Covenant. There will be no need to sprinkle blood on His throne. King Messiah already shed His blood and sprinkled it in the holy place in heaven forever. The "blood" is sitting on the "Mercy Seat" which is the throne of David.

The blood being placed on the outside of the temple is symbolic of what King Messiah had accomplished on the cross. The blood placed on the gate of the inner court will be a witness to all who pass by of the shed blood of Jesus for sin.

The Day of Atonement was fulfilled at the first coming of the Lord Jesus. The temple on earth was just a type of the one in heaven. It is the shed blood of King Messiah sprinkled in the heavenly temple which reconciled man to the holy God of Israel. The temple on earth is the shadow, while the one in heaven is real. The Book of Hebrews shows this:

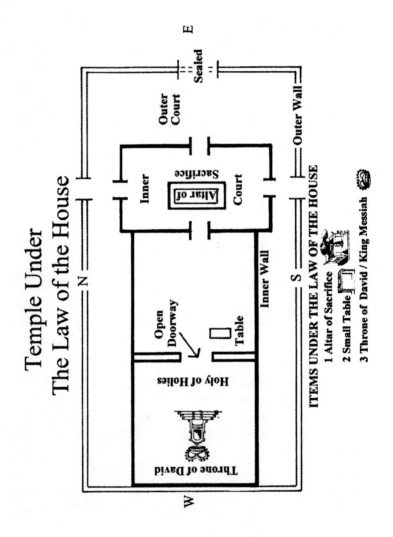

Temple Under The Law of the House

ITEMS UNDER THE LAW OF THE HOUSE

1 Altar of Sacrifice
2 Small Table
3 Throne of David / King Messiah

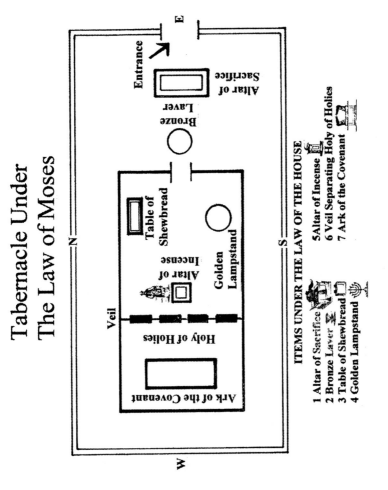

> Hebrews 9:11 "But Christ being come an high priest of good things to come, by a greater and more perfect tabernacle, not made with hands, that is to say, not of this building; (12) Neither by the blood of goats and calves, but by his own blood he entered in once into the holy place, having obtained eternal redemption for us."

Thus the reconciliation of the temple in Ezekiel 45:18-20 is a memorial to the shed blood of the Lord Jesus. It will be a visible witness to the people that they are already reconciled. God does not require perfection, but a willing heart. The reconciliation of His house shows the people are free to come before Him even if they have made an error. Remember, the Lord Jesus is going to be in His glory. It could be difficult for people, who are born during His reign, to accept that God is not against them if they do something foolish.

Think forward to the time when the Lord is reigning in His glory in His magnificent temple. It could be difficult for people to accept that if they do something foolish they can be reconciled with God who is in His glory seated on His throne. The rituals of the law of the temple are visible proof to the people at this time that they are reconciled with God. They do not have to feel separated from Him.

CHAPTER SIX

Sin During the Reign of the Lord Jesus

"And so thou shalt do the seventh day of the month for every one that erreth, and for him that is simple: so shall ye reconcile the house." Ezekiel 45:20

To understand that the sacrifices in the temple are memorials, it is important to understand the living environment under the Lord Jesus. The world is going to be radically different than now to the point it will be unrecognizable. Sin will not be the problem then as it is now.

The world system that promotes sin, greed, immorality and rebellion against God will have been destroyed. This system is known as Babylon and will be destroyed by God just prior to the second coming of the Lord Jesus. Satan will have been bound and there will be no deception. There will be no false gods and false religions to lead people away from the holy God of Israel. Righteousness and holiness will cover the earth. There will be no false gods and false religions; only the name of the LORD will be known in that day.

Satan bound and no deception:

> Revelation 20:2 "And he laid hold on the dragon, that old serpent, which is the Devil, and Satan, and bound him a thousand years, (3) And cast him into the bottomless pit, and shut him up, and set a seal upon him, that he should deceive the nations no more..."

The destruction of the corrupt world system:

> Revelation 14:8 "And there followed another angel, saying, Babylon is fallen, is fallen, that great city, because she made all nations drink of the wine of the wrath of her fornication."

Only the LORD's name known:

> Zechariah 14:9 "And the LORD shall be king over all the earth: in that day shall there be one LORD, and his name one."

At the second coming of the Lord Jesus, Israel will be purged of its sin. The nation will be holy, as the Holy Spirit and the word will be placed in the peoples' hearts. Israel will be called a holy nation when the people are purged from their sin and rebellion against the LORD.

> Isaiah 4:3 "And it shall come to pass, that he that is left in Zion, and he that remaineth in Jerusalem, shall be called holy...(4) When the Lord shall have washed away the filth of the daughters of Zion, and shall have purged the blood of Jerusalem from the midst thereof by the spirit of judgment, and by the spirit of burning."

The final cleansing of Israel will take place when God cleanses Israel by the Holy Spirit and creates a new spiritual heart in the people. This action brings Israel under the New Covenant. The ritual of Yom Kippur could not permanently cleanse the people, but the action of the Holy Spirit will. God's Spirit in the heart of the people will cause them to walk in His statutes and keep His law.

> Ezekiel 36:25-27 "Then will I sprinkle clean water upon you, and ye shall be clean: from all your filthiness, and from all your idols, will I cleanse you.
>
> (26) A new heart also will I give you, and a new spirit will I put within you: and I will take away the stony heart out of your flesh, and I will give you an heart of flesh. (27) And I will put my spirit within you, and cause you to walk in my statutes, and ye shall keep my judgments, and do them."

The Bible is very clear that at the time when King Messiah is ruling from His throne that the people will not follow the imaginations of an evil heart. With the presence of King Messiah in the midst of the nations, man's bent to do evil will have been dealt with by the new heart.

> Jeremiah 3:17 "At that time they shall call Jerusalem the throne of the LORD; and all the nations shall be gathered unto it, to the name of the LORD, to Jerusalem: neither shall they walk any more after the imagination of their evil heart."

One of the conditions for the LORD to dwell in His glory in the midst of His people is that they will not walk after the imaginations of an evil heart. The people will not commit iniquity nor will they lie or use deceit. This is a radical change from the present condition of the human heart.

> Zephaniah 3:13 "The remnant of Israel shall not do iniquity, nor speak lies; neither shall a deceitful tongue be found in their mouth: for they shall feed and lie down, and none shall make them afraid."

Israel will be holy before the LORD at this time. Israel will be called "The holy people." Jerusalem shall be the holy city. The people, Jerusalem, and Mount Zion will all be holy. Everything connected with Israel and Jerusalem will be holy.

> Isaiah 62:11-12 "Behold, the LORD hath proclaimed unto the end of the world, Say ye to the daughter of Zion, Behold, thy salvation cometh; behold, his reward is with him, and his work before him. (12) And they shall call them, The holy people, The redeemed of the LORD: and thou shalt be called, Sought out, A city not forsaken."
> Joel 3:17 "So shall ye know that I am the LORD your God dwelling in Zion, my holy mountain: then shall Jerusalem be holy, and there shall no strangers pass through her any more."

Under the reign of the Lord Jesus, people will have perfect conditions. He will be reigning in His glory. Satan will have been bound. The corrupt world system will have been destroyed. There will be no false gods, teachers or prophets. The people will have been given a new heart and the Holy Spirit will empower them to keep God's word. Sin is not going to be a major issue at that time as it is now.

Thus the Bible shows that the condition for God dwelling in the midst of Israel will be that sin has been dealt with and it is no longer an issue. The people will have been purged of their sin and will not commit the iniquity that brings defilement. This is the condition that God set for dwelling in the midst of the people forever. The putting away of iniquity is a prerequisite for the holy God of Israel to dwell in Jerusalem:

> Ezekiel 43:7 "And he said unto me, Son of man, the place of my throne, and the place of the soles of my feet, where I will dwell in the midst of the children of Israel for ever, and my holy name, shall the house of Israel no more defile, neither they, nor their kings, by their whoredom, nor by the carcases of their kings in their high places.
>
> (8) In their setting of their threshold by my thresholds, and their post by my posts, and the wall between me and them, they have even defiled my holy name by their abominations that they have committed: wherefore I have consumed them in mine anger.
>
> (9) Now let them put away their whoredom, and the carcases of their kings, far from me, and I will dwell in the midst of them for ever."

When the Lord is reigning from His holy house on holy Mount Zion with His holy law of the temple, sin as it is today is not going to be a factor. God would not tolerate iniquity in His presence and the fact that King Messiah is seated on His throne in His glory means the sin of man will have been dealt with. The people will be holy exactly like the Bible states, and King Messiah will dwell in their midst in His glory. God will have provided everything needed for the people to be holy, to live holy and to stay holy.

The sin mentioned under the law of the temple will be considered just errors and acting simple. As a result, the law of the temple does not have any remedy for rebellion against the LORD. God recognizes that people are not perfect, and the rituals are to show they are forgiven of these shortcomings. The sin will be error and doing stupid things and not open rebellion against God's word.

> Ezekiel 45:20 "And so thou shalt do the seventh day of the month for every one that erreth, and for him that is simple: so shall ye reconcile the house."

Man will have the perfect environment to live in under the rule of King Messiah; however, those born during this time will have the ability to sin. There will still be free will. Man will have the ability to willfully rebel against God's word. The law of the temple does not have any remedy for this rebellion. The Bible states that at this time King Messiah will be ruling with a rod of iron.

> Revelation 19:15 "And out of his mouth goeth a sharp sword, that with it he should smite the nations: and he shall rule them with a rod of iron: and he treadeth the winepress of the fierceness and wrath of Almighty God."

The person who sins and rebels against Him will be swiftly dealt with. Willful sin will not be tolerated and the sinner will suffer immediate physical and spiritual death. Fornication, adultery, homosexuality, murder, etc. will not be tolerated at this time. The person who willfully sins with the perfect conditions God has arranged will be accursed and doomed. There is no more sacrifice for these types of sins during the reign of King Messiah. God will not tolerate iniquity during this time. The prophet Isaiah states as follows:

> Isaiah 65:20 "There shall be no more thence an infant of days, nor an old man that hath not filled his days: for the child shall die an hundred years old; **but the sinner being an hundred years old shall be accursed.**"

Keep in mind, at this time, God in the person of King Messiah in His glory will be ruling from His throne. His physical glory is going to be seen all over the earth. People will have the visible witness to the glory of God and the authority of His word on earth. Willful sin will not be condoned in the presence of the glory of God. The following verse shows that the glory of the Lord will affect the entire earth:

> Ezekiel 43:2 "and, behold, the glory of the God of Israel came from the way of the east: and his voice was like a noise of many waters: and the earth shined with his glory."

Before man first sinned through Adam, the sin was committed when he could come into the direct presence of God. This would mean Adam saw God in His glory. Man was judged when he sinned. This judgment was both spiritual and physical death. Man, in the sinful state, was then blocked from the presence of the LORD.

God redeemed man through the shed blood of the Lord Jesus on the cross. This was a tremendous price He paid to redeem man. God will not tolerate any willful sin when He is ruling as King Messiah in His glory, but He will deal with man's weaknesses or errors and foolishness. But, the person who willfully sins will be accursed.

There is no indication under the law of the temple there is a reversing of this curse. As a result, should any person willfully sin during the reign of King Messiah, it will mean the immediate removal of that person from the presence of God's glory. This will mean physical and spiritual death.

There is no remedy for an accursed person under the law of the temple. Since, at this time, the church has been completed and the Lord Jesus is reigning on earth, where can the cursed person go but to hell and separation from the holy God of Israel? The accursed person is to be cut off which means death.

> Psalms 37:22 "For such as be blessed of him shall inherit the earth; and they that be cursed of him shall be cut off."

Both the law of Moses and the New Testament give a frightful picture of being accursed for breaking God's word. Under the law, the accursed person was to be killed and hung on a tree for all to see. There was no hope for anyone accursed of God. This is reserved for people with hardened hearts against God. The book of Deuteronomy shows this:

> Deuteronomy 21:22 "And if a man have committed a sin worthy of death, and he be to be put to death, and thou hang him on a tree:
> (23) His body shall not remain all night upon the tree, but thou shalt in any wise bury him that day; (for he that is hanged is accursed of God;) that thy land be not defiled, which the LORD thy God giveth thee for an inheritance."

In the New Testament, the person who preaches a false gospel is to be accursed. The Greek word for accursed is anathema which is a very strong word. The word accursed is defined as *to consign to destruction with a curse.* A willful sinner under the law of the temple will be given over to destruction.

The sacrifices in the law of the temple are for holy people that have committed an error or acted simple. These sacrifices have nothing to do with hard-core sin, transgression and iniquity. These types of sins cause the person to be accursed of God; therefore, that person cannot be reconciled under the law of the temple.

The severity of being accursed is seen by the judgment on false preachers. The strongest possible condemnation falls on them, as they are accursed.

> Galatians 1:8 "But though we, or an angel from heaven, preach any other gospel unto you than that which we have preached unto you, let him be accursed. (9) As we said before, so say I now again, If any man preach any other gospel unto you than that ye have received, let him be accursed."

During this time, willful sin will be very rare. Holiness will be the standard all over the earth. Satan will be bound and deception and temptations removed. The corrupt world system will have been destroyed. Man will have been given a new spiritual heart with the filling of the Holy Spirit. Sin will not be as it is now. It will be very rare and immediately judged.

The law of the temple will deal with the errors and foolishness of people and not the hard-core rebellion of sinners. King Messiah will use the rod of iron to deal with a sinner in rebellion against His authority and holiness.

With God in His glory sitting on the throne, it will be very difficult for the new born people to comprehend that He died for sin and brought in the New Covenant. People could feel inadequate before Him when committing an error and acting simple. The blood placed on the outside of the temple and on the inner court will be a visible sign that all has been reconciled by what He did on the cross. When King Messiah teaches the law of the temple, the people will see clearly how the rituals all point to what He did on the cross.

CHAPTER SEVEN

The New Covenant and the Law of the Temple

"For this is my blood of the new testament (covenant), which is shed for many for the remission of sins." Matthew 26:28

The vast differences between the law of Moses and the law of the temple can only be explained through the New Covenant. These changes could only occur with a change in the law. It is impossible to reconcile the law of Moses with the law of the temple. The following is a partial list of the differences that cannot be reconciled.

Under the law of the temple:

There is no Aaronic high priest.
There is no Yom Kippur.
The blood of reconciliation is placed on the outside of the temple and inner court.
The temple is reconciled only for errors and foolishness and not iniquity, transgression and willful sin.

There is no veil of separation of the most holy place.
There is no menorah, table of shew bread, brazen laver or altar of incense.
The Ark of the Covenant is replaced by the throne of the God of Israel.
The Messiah sits on the throne as both King and High Priest.

Jeremiah shows that a New Covenant would replace the law of Moses. This covenant would not be like the one God made at Mt. Sinai. This covenant would be so powerful that the sin problem between man and God would be resolved, and the knowledge of God would cover the earth.

This covenant would be vastly different than the one at Sinai. It would cause God to forgive iniquity and not remember it! Under the law of Moses, continual sacrifice had to be made for sin which means it was not forgotten by God. The New Covenant is so powerful that it would cause God not to remember sin! With this covenant, God would touch the very heart of man by placing His word in people's heart. The Scriptures from the book of Jeremiah follow:

> Jeremiah 31:31 "Behold, the days come, saith the LORD, that I will make a new covenant with the house of Israel, and with the house of Judah: (32) Not according to the covenant that I made with their fathers in the day that I took them by the hand to bring them out of the land of Egypt; which my covenant they brake, although I was an husband unto them, saith the LORD:
> (33) But this shall be the covenant that I will make with the house of Israel; After those days, saith the LORD, I will put my law in their inward parts, and write it in their

hearts; and will be their God, and they shall be my people.

(34) And they shall teach no more every man his neighbour, and every man his brother, saying, Know the LORD: for they shall all know me, from the least of them unto the greatest of them, saith the LORD: for I will forgive their iniquity, and I will remember their sin no more."

Ezekiel shows that at the initiation of Israel coming under the New Covenant, the people will be purged of sin and uncleanness. Under the New Covenant, Israel will be holy and will obey and keep God's statutes and judgments. The reason God's word can be kept is the Spirit of God will be placed in the heart of man. This is radically different from the law of Moses.

Ezekiel 36:25 "Then will I sprinkle clean water upon you, and ye shall be clean: from all your filthiness, and from all your idols, will I cleanse you. (26) A new heart also will I give you, and a new spirit will I put within you: and I will take away the stony heart out of your flesh, and I will give you an heart of flesh. (27) **And I will put my spirit within you**, and cause you to walk in my statutes, and ye shall keep my judgments, and do them."

The sinful human heart will be replaced under this covenant with a heart that is powered by God's Spirit. Without the New Covenant, God says that the human heart is like a stone. Under the New Covenant, God calls it a heart of flesh. After God purges Israel of sin, the nation becomes holy. God then refers to Israel as the holy people.

> Isaiah 4:3 "And it shall come to pass, that he that is left in Zion, and he that remaineth in Jerusalem, shall be **called holy**, even every one that is written among the living in Jerusalem: (4) When the Lord shall have washed away the filth of the daughters of Zion, and shall have purged the blood of Jerusalem from the midst thereof by the spirit of judgment, and by the spirit of burning."
>
> Isaiah 62:12 "And they shall call them, The **holy people**, The redeemed of the LORD..."

Isaiah shows that the New Covenant is a person. The New Covenant is made with God's righteous Servant. Zechariah identified God's Servant as the Branch and, through the Branch, sin would be dealt with in one day! God's Servant is His righteous King, the Branch of David. The Scriptures from Zechariah that show this follow:

> Zechariah 3:8 "Hear now, O Joshua the high priest, thou, and thy fellows that sit before thee: for they are men wondered at: for, behold, I will bring forth **my servant** the BRANCH.
>
> (9) For behold the stone that I have laid before Joshua; upon one stone shall be seven eyes: behold, I will engrave the graving thereof, saith the LORD of hosts, and **I will remove the iniquity of that land in one day.**"

This is a most important concept to grasp. The New Covenant is a person called God's Servant, the Branch. When Israel comes under the New Covenant, the people will come under the direct authority of King Messiah. When God places His Spirit in the heart of the people, the Messiah will do it. When God remembers sin no more, it is because of the New Covenant with King Messiah. Isaiah shows the New Covenant is the person of God's Servant:

> Isaiah 42:1,6 "Behold my servant, whom I uphold; mine elect, in whom my soul delighteth; I have put my spirit upon him: he shall bring forth judgment to the Gentiles. (6) I the LORD have called thee in righteousness, and will hold thine hand, and will keep thee, and **give thee for a covenant** of the people, for a light of the Gentiles..."
>
> Isaiah 49:8 "Thus saith the LORD, In an acceptable time have I heard thee, and in a day of salvation have I helped thee: and I will preserve thee, and **give thee for a covenant** of the people, to establish the earth, to cause to inherit the desolate heritages..."

The prophet Isaiah clearly states what the Messiah is going to accomplish so that God will remember sin no more. Isaiah chapter 53, with great detail, shows the ministry of God's righteous Servant, King Messiah, to establish the New Covenant. The New Covenant will be based on the death of God's Servant for sin. He will pay the price for sin to reconcile sinful man with the holy God of Israel. This is exactly what Jesus of Nazareth did to establish the New Covenant. These verses follow:

> Isaiah 53:6 "All we like sheep have gone astray; we have turned every one to his own way; and the LORD hath laid on him the iniquity of us all...(11) He shall see of the travail of his soul, and shall be satisfied: by his knowledge shall my righteous servant justify

many; for he shall bear their iniquities."

1 Peter 2:24 "Who his own self bare our sins in his own body on the tree, that we, being dead to sins, should live unto righteousness: by whose stripes ye were healed."

1 Peter 3:18 "For Christ also hath once suffered for sins, the just for the unjust, that he might bring us to God, being put to death in the flesh, but quickened by the Spirit:"

The New Covenant was established 2000 years ago when the Lord Jesus died on the cross and shed His blood to reconcile sinful man with the holy God of Israel. This covenant is in force at the present time. God now deals with both the Jews and Gentiles through the New Covenant and not the law of Moses.

Hebrews 13:20 "Now the God of peace, that brought again from the dead our Lord Jesus, that great shepherd of the sheep, through the blood of the everlasting covenant..."

Romans 1:16 "For I am not ashamed of the gospel of Christ: for it is the power of God unto salvation to every one that believeth; to the Jew first, and also to the Greek."

Israel as a nation rejected the Lord Jesus at His first coming. When the LORD has completed building His church, Israel will once again be the center of His attention. God has not forsaken Israel, but in the near future God will have Israel as the focus of His attention. He will deal with the nations through His people Israel.

Under the New Covenant, Israel will be made holy. This will occur when God purges the people of their sin and uncleanness by His Holy Spirit. God will pour out His Spirit on the people and give them a new heart and put His Spirit within them. This will enable the people to walk in God's statutes and keep His word. All this will happen at the second coming of the Lord Jesus when Israel comes to recognize Him as the Branch of David, their King Messiah. The spirit of grace and supplications will be given to Israel when the Lord Jesus is recognized as the one who died for them.

> Zechariah 12:10 "And I will pour upon the house of David, and upon the inhabitants of Jerusalem, the spirit of grace and of supplications: and they shall look upon me whom they have pierced, and they shall mourn for him, as one mourneth for his only son..."

The law of Moses could be changed because it only pointed to what King Messiah was going to do. The law of Moses could not remit sin as year after year the blood was taken into the temple and sprinkled on the Ark of the Covenant. Remember, the Ark will be replaced by the throne of God, Jeremiah 3:16,17. However, under the law of the temple, the blood is placed on the outside of the temple because of the New Covenant. The throne is in the most holy place with King Messiah seated on it. There is no need for Yom Kippur under the law of the temple.

Under the New Covenant, there is no need for a menorah in the temple because it only pointed to the Messiah as the light of the world. All the articles in the tabernacle will not be needed under the law of the temple. King Messiah seated on His throne could only be possible under the New Covenant.

He will be sitting on the throne as both King and High Priest. The law of Moses could never allow this. Under the New Covenant, the Messiah can be both King and High Priest because it is based on the oath of God, Psalm 2:6,7 and

Psalm 110:1,4. Because the priesthood was changed under the law of the temple, there has to be a change in the law.

> Hebrews 7:12 "For the priesthood being changed, there is made of necessity a change also of the law."

The change is that the law of the temple is under the New Covenant that was instituted by the Lord Jesus when He died on the cross for the redemption of man. The law of the temple reflects the New Covenant and not the covenant under the law of Moses.

The radical changes in the law of the temple can only be explained by the operation of the New Covenant. When the law shall go forth from Jerusalem and King Messiah is teaching the law, He will be teaching the law of the temple under the New Covenant.

The house of the LORD will be an object lesson for the people about the teachings of the New Covenant. All the articles of the tabernacle in the wilderness pointed to the Messiah. They can be viewed as types or shadows and as temporary. Under the New Covenant, the reality of the types is seated on the throne of David. The law of the temple is then the New Covenant under the reign of the Lord Jesus, King Messiah. This is the law and the word that the LORD will teach from Jerusalem.

> Isaiah 2:3 "And many people shall go and say, Come ye, and let us go up to the mountain of the LORD, to the house of the God of Jacob; and he will teach us of his ways, and we will walk in his paths: for out of Zion shall go forth the law, and the word of the LORD from Jerusalem."

CHAPTER EIGHT

The "Prince" of Ezekiel 45

"And it shall be the prince's part to give burnt offerings, and meat offerings, and drink offerings, in the feasts, and in the new moons, and in the Sabbaths, in all solemnities of the house of Israel: he shall prepare the sin offering, and the meat offering, and the burnt offering, and the peace offerings, to make reconciliation for the house of Israel."
Ezekiel 45:17

The Bible gives special attention to one prince during the Messiah's reign. This prince cannot be the Messiah because the Messiah will be seated on His throne in Ezekiel 43:7. The Bible never identifies this prince, but it is important to show that he is not King Messiah.

This prince never sits on a throne. In fact, Ezekiel 44:2-3 clearly indicates that this prince will be only permitted to enter by the way of the porch of the East gate and eat bread before the LORD. The Messiah will reside in the temple seated on His throne. The Bible shows that during the reign of King Messiah there will be only one throne in the temple, not two. There is no indication of a second throne. There is only one throne and this is in the most holy place, Ezekiel 43:7. This is not the throne of the prince, but it is for the LORD, King Messiah. The Scriptures to show that the prince will only come before the throne follow:

> Ezekiel 44:2 "Then said the LORD unto me; This gate shall be shut, it shall not be opened, and no man shall enter in by it; because the LORD, the God of Israel, hath entered in by it, therefore it shall be shut.
>
> (3) It is for the prince; the prince, he shall sit in it to eat bread before the LORD; he shall enter by the way of the porch of that gate, and shall go out by the way of the same."

Since the prince of Ezekiel 45:17 does not sit on a throne, he cannot be the Messiah. According to Ezekiel 44:2,3, it is this prince who only approaches the throne. The Messiah will be the King sitting upon the throne of David. By realizing that King Messiah is sitting on His throne, according to Ezekiel 43:7, it becomes clear that the prince cannot be the Messiah.

One other area to look at to show that this prince is not the Messiah is the inheritance of land. Ezekiel 45 lists the land that this prince will inherit during the Messianic reign. He will inherit a small parcel of land near the temple. This is the entire land granted to this prince. These Scriptures follow:

> Ezekiel 45:6 "And ye shall appoint the possession of the city five thousand broad, and five and twenty thousand long, over against the oblation of the holy portion: it shall be for the whole house of Israel. (7) And a portion shall be for the prince on the

one side and on the other side of the oblation
of the holy portion..."

Notice in verse seven the prince only receives a tiny portion
of land. Is this the land for Messiah, the King over all the
earth? Psalms 2 clearly states that the Messiah will inherit
the entire earth, not just a small parcel of land in the nation
of Israel:

> Psalms 2:6 "Yet have I set my king upon my
> holy hill of Zion. (7) I will declare the
> decree: the LORD hath said unto me, Thou
> art my Son; this day have I begotten thee.
> (8) Ask of me, and I shall give thee the
> heathen for thine inheritance, and the utter-
> most parts of the earth for thy possession."

The contrast between the possession of land for the prince
of Ezekiel 45:6-7, and the Messiah in Psalm 2:8 is remark-
able. The Messiah, the King of the world, receives the utter-
most parts of the earth for his possession. On the other hand,
the prince of Ezekiel 45:6-7 receives a small parcel of land
in Jerusalem.

The Prince of Ezekiel 45 will be special before the
LORD, but he is not King Messiah. Although the identity of
this prince is not known, it is clear that he will not be King
Messiah.

Part Two

How to be Dressed in King Messiah's Presence

CHAPTER NINE

If Thou Doest Well,
Shalt Thou not be Accepted

Genesis 4:6 "And the LORD said unto Cain,
Why art thou wroth? and why is thy counte-
nance fallen? (7) If thou doest well, shalt
thou not be accepted? and if thou doest not
well, sin lieth at the door. And unto thee shall
be his desire, and thou shalt rule over him."

Genesis chapter four is a story that almost everyone is
familiar with. The story revolves around two brothers
named Cain and Abel. One brother, Abel, approached God
with the best of his flock of sheep and was accepted while
Cain brought the harvest of his crops and was rejected. Cain
eventually grew to hate his brother and murdered him. This
chapter is more than just a story. Chapter four is showcasing
a very important Biblical concept.

This chapter sets the foundation on how to approach
God, and how He deals with man's sin. Other sections of the
Bible build upon this chapter. The clear way to obey God is
taught in the story of Cain and Abel.

To understand this chapter, you first have to realize what happened in the relationship between God and man in the previous three chapters. Chapter one records the creation of all things, including man. While creating, the Bible records six times God stated, "It was good." The last act of creation was man. After creating man, God then states, "It was very good." There is no mention of death or sin at this time, and no form of worship was mentioned.

> Genesis 1:31 "And God saw every thing that he had made, and, behold, it was very good. And the evening and the morning were the sixth day."

In chapter two, God first mentions death. Man was warned not to rebel against God's word or he would die. Here is the first mention of death in the Bible, and it is directly tied to sin. There is a severe penalty for sin and that is death. There is a cause and effect relationship between sin and death. The physical act of sin brought both physical and spiritual death to man. Spiritual death means eternal separation from the holy God of Israel.

The correlation between sin and death is an extremely important concept to understanding why God instituted the sacrificial system. Genesis chapter two then becomes foundational to show the effect of rebellion against God's word. Both the Old and New Testament make a direct correlation between sin and death. The Scriptures to show this follow:

> Genesis 2:17 "But of the tree of the knowledge of good and evil, thou shalt not eat of it: for in the day that thou eatest thereof thou shalt surely die."
> Romans 6:23 "For the wages of sin is death..."

In chapter three, another very important foundational concept of Scripture was made evident. Adam's sin alienated all of mankind from God. Man rebelled against God and sinned. The rebellion brought immediate judgment from God and fellowship between man and God was broken. Man came under the penalty of sin which was death.

The immediate death was spiritual as Adam and Eve were driven from the presence of the LORD and no longer had direct access to God in the Garden of Eden. Adam's spiritual death was immediate while the physical death came later.

Adam's sin had a devastating effect on all of mankind. The effect of Adam's sin had consequences to today. When Adam was banished from the presence of God, all of mankind was banished. Adam could be looked at as the federal head of mankind and what he did affected everyone.

This banishment of mankind from God's presence can be seen in Adam being driven from the Garden. When Adam was driven away, a block was put at the Garden so no one could enter. Adam was blocked so he could not obtain eternal life in the Garden. This prevented him from obtaining eternal life in a sinful state which would mean eternal separation from God.

It was not only Adam who was banished but all of mankind. Following Adam in the Bible were Abel and Noah. They were also blocked from entering the Garden because of what Adam did. Adam's sin had dire consequences for all of mankind. There are those that do not believe mankind had inherited a sin nature. The Bible shows through the fall of Adam and his subsequent banning from the Garden of Eden that all mankind inherited his sin nature.

The New Testament is in perfect agreement with this issue. The sin of Adam was passed to all mankind. Adam's sin has touched all of mankind to this day. The Scriptures to show the Garden was blocked to all of mankind follow:

> Genesis 3:22 "And the LORD God said, Behold, the man is become as one of us, to know good and evil: and now, lest he put forth his hand, and take also of the tree of life, and eat, and live for ever: (23) Therefore the LORD God sent him forth from the garden of Eden, to till the ground from whence he was taken.
>
> (24) So he drove out the man; and he placed at the east of the garden of Eden Cherubims, and a flaming sword which turned every way, to keep the way of the tree of life."
>
> Romans 5:12 "Wherefore, as by one man sin entered into the world, and death by sin; and so death passed upon all men, for that all have sinned: (14) Nevertheless death reigned from Adam to Moses, even over them that had not sinned after the similitude of Adam's transgression..."

The principle that all of mankind inherited the sin nature from Adam was established from the beginning at the fall. In the first chapter of Genesis, 10 times in five verses, God said that everything was to reproduce after its own kind. This is a basic law. Dogs reproduce dogs, etc. When Adam fell into sin, his nature was passed on to his offspring. He reproduced offspring after his own kind which meant they had the sin nature just like he did. All of mankind came under the sin nature of Adam.

> Genesis 1:25 "And God made the beast of the earth after his kind, and cattle after their kind, and every thing that creepeth upon the earth after his kind: and God saw that it was good.

> (28) And God blessed them, and God said
> unto them, Be fruitful, and multiply, and
> replenish the earth..."

God had commanded man to be fruitful and fill the earth. This meant to reproduce after his kind. Adam, in this fallen state of sin, reproduced people with his sin nature. He was reproducing after his kind. Everyone who has a human father has to be born with the sin nature that is traced directly back to Adam.

As a consequence of Adam's sin, He hid before the presence of God. God reached out to him. God sought Adam and promised that fellowship would be restored. God told Adam that a confrontation would come and the seed of the woman would triumph over the evil which had seduced him. At this point, God did not give details of how this victory would occur nor how long it would take. He simply stated that man, through the seed of the woman, would be victorious over evil.

God did say the victory would entail violence, and there would be a physical confrontation between the seed of the woman and the seed of evil. The seed of the woman would crush the evil. This verse follows:

> Genesis 3:15 "And I will put enmity between
> thee and the woman, and between thy seed
> and her seed; it shall bruise thy head, and
> thou shalt bruise his heel."

Immediately after man sinned, the Bible records the first physical death. Man was now physically naked and needed to be clothed. The Bible records that God made coats of animal skins and clothed them. To make clothes of animal skins required the death of the animals. The first deaths in the Bible were to cover man because of sin.

123

Genesis 3:21 "Unto Adam also and to his wife did the LORD God make coats of skins, and clothed them."

In examining Genesis chapters one, two and three some very important principles are established. These principles carry through the entire Bible and set the stage for the study of chapter four. When examining the Bible and especially the need for sacrifices, these principles must always be kept in mind. The principles follow:

There is a penalty for sin which is death.
There is a direct relationship between sin and death.
Adam died spiritually the moment he sinned.
Sin brought immediate judgment from God which meant spiritual separation from Him.
Everything reproduces after its own kind; therefore sinful man reproduced offspring with the sin nature.
All of mankind came under the sin of Adam and were prevented from entering the Garden of Eden for eternal life.
Man's sin caused the first physical death. Animals were slain for clothes to cover man.
God promised that man could be delivered from the sin.

God's Remedy For Overcoming Sin

God's remedy for overcoming sin was in His worship system as seen in Genesis 4:1-8. The word sin is used for the very first time in this section of Scripture. There was no recorded worship system established in the Bible prior to this chapter; however, Abel knew to bring the best of the sheep before the Lord.

It is obvious that God had established a system prior to this because Abel knew to bring the best of the sheep before God. Perhaps when God told Adam about the coming redemption from sin, He also established the system. Or, maybe when He slew the animals for garments, Adam was told about God's method for dealing with man's sin. The Bible does not say when the system was established, but it was in force at the time of Cain and Abel. The verses to show this follow:

> Genesis 4:3 "And in process of time it came to pass, that Cain brought of the fruit of the ground an offering unto the LORD.
>
> (4) And Abel, he also brought of the firstlings of his flock and of the fat thereof. And the LORD had respect unto Abel and to his offering"

There is no mention at this time of sacrifice. The Bible simply states that Cain brought fruit of the ground as an offering while Abel brought the best of his sheep. At this point, there is no mention of clean or unclean animals or sacrifice for sin. The Bible does not even mention why the offerings were brought before God. Cain and Abel just did it.

Later in Genesis, Noah adds more to this. Noah knew about the clean and unclean animals. He was told to bring two of all kinds of animals into the Ark, but of the clean animals he was told by God to bring in seven pairs. There is no indication in the Bible how Noah knew the clean from the unclean.

The Bible does not tell us what were the clean animals,

but Noah knew the clean from the unclean. This was long before Moses and the law. From the very beginning, the time of Adam and Eve, man knew about God's worship system of sacrifices and why God required them. The Scripture to show the clean and unclean animals follows:

> Genesis 7:2 "Of every clean beast thou shalt take to thee by sevens, the male and his female: and of beasts that are not clean by two, the male and his female."

After the flood, the very first thing Noah built was an altar to the LORD and offered sacrifices. These sacrifices were called burnt offerings. This is seen in Genesis 8. The Bible does not indicate that Noah was commanded to do this. It does not indicate when he was instructed about building an altar and offering sacrifices. He simply knew to do it. He knew to offer only the clean animals as sacrifices to the LORD. The Bible goes on to say that the offerings of the clean animals touched the very heart of God!

These verses show the importance of sacrificing clean animals to the LORD because it touches His heart! The Bible is very clear that burnt offerings touched the very heart of God. These verses are critical to understanding why God instituted sacrifices. The verses to show this follow:

> Genesis 8:20 "And Noah builded an altar unto the LORD; and took of every clean beast, and of every clean fowl, and offered burnt offerings on the altar.
>
> (21) And the LORD smelled a sweet savour; and the LORD said in his heart, I will not again curse the ground any more for man's sake; for the imagination of man's heart is evil from his youth; neither will I

again smite any more every thing living, as I have done."

The Bible is clear that God instituted burnt offerings, and this ritual was not the invention of man. Job was well aware of the need for burnt offerings for sin. He continually offered burnt offerings for his family in case they had sinned. Job knew the direct connection between burnt offerings for sin and touching the heart of God.

> Job 1:5 "And it was so, when the days of their feasting were gone about, that Job sent and sanctified them, and rose up early in the morning, and offered burnt offerings according to the number of them all: for Job said, It may be that my sons have sinned, and cursed God in their hearts. Thus did Job continually."

Close friends gave Job false counsel. Some of this counsel involved a false understanding of God. When Job's time of testing was complete, God revealed Himself to Job. One thing God addressed was the false counsel about Him that Job was given by his friends, Eliphaz, Bildad and Zophar. God Himself stated the remedy for this sin of false counsel was to offer burnt offerings. The burnt offerings were seven bullocks and seven rams.

The key to this is that God Himself initiated the need for burnt offerings to atone for sin. It is clear that the idea of sacrifice for atonement, or payment for sin's penalty was initiated by God Himself at the very time Adam sinned. Abel, Noah, Abraham and Job all knew the need for the clean animals and burnt offerings and this was long before the law of Moses. The verses to show God initiated burnt offerings with Job's counselors follow:

Job 42: 7 "And it was so, that after the LORD had spoken these words unto Job, the LORD said to Eliphaz the Temanite, My wrath is kindled against thee, and against thy two friends: for ye have not spoken of me the thing that is right, as my servant Job hath.

(8) Therefore take unto you now seven bullocks and seven rams, and go to my servant Job, and offer up for yourselves **a burnt offering**; and my servant Job shall pray for you: for him will I accept: lest I deal with you after your folly, in that ye have not spoken of me the thing which is right, like my servant Job.

(9) So Eliphaz the Temanite and Bildad the Shuhite and Zophar the Naamathite went, and did according as the LORD commanded them: the LORD also accepted Job."

Genesis 8 was the first time recorded in the Bible that an animal was sacrificed. This chapter tells us why God wanted the clean animals sacrificed. This process touches God's heart and causes Him to overlook judgment for sin.

Verse 21 shows that the sacrifices cause Him to stop the judgment for sin. The sacrifices allow God to deal with man and his sin nature. The verse actually mentions man's sin nature: "For the imagination of man's heart is evil from his youth." This nature was inherited directly from Adam.

There are very few things recorded in the Bible that touch the heart of God. Two of them are found with Noah. The first is the sin of man. It grieved God in His heart that He had to judge the earth at the time of Noah. Man was wicked and continually violent. This wickedness and violence grieved God in His heart, and He had to move in judgment. Sin touches the very heart of God.

The next is the burnt offerings made by Noah. The burnt offerings of the clean animals were a sweet savor to God. These sacrifices touched God's heart about man's sin nature and caused Him not to execute judgment for sin. This is the most important concept to grasp. The burnt offerings touched God's heart regarding man's sin. The verses to show this follow:

> Genesis 6:5 "And God saw that the wickedness of man was great in the earth, and that every imagination of the thoughts of his heart was only evil continually. (6) And it repented the LORD that he had made man on the earth, and **it grieved him at his heart.**"
> Genesis 8:20 "And Noah builded an altar unto the LORD; and took of every clean beast, and of every clean fowl, and offered burnt offerings on the altar. (21) And the LORD smelled a sweet savour; and **the LORD said in his heart,** I will not again curse the ground any more for man's sake; for the imagination of man's heart is evil from his youth; neither will I again smite any more every thing living, as I have done."

Man sinned and brought upon himself the penalty of death, and the Bible is clear that the death of the clean animals paid that penalty. Later in the Bible there were others who offered burnt offerings.

Abraham and Job offered burnt offerings and in the law of Moses there are numerous times burnt offerings were made. In fact, burnt offerings are a central part of the rituals under the law of Moses. All those burnt offerings touched the heart of God just as the burnt offerings that Noah had made. It was the burnt offerings of only the clean animals that touched the heart of God.

Later in the Bible the clean animals are identified. These animals would include: heifers, bullocks, sheep, goats, doves and pigeons. The Bible says that Noah sacrificed burnt offerings of every clean animal and bird so Noah would have offered at least one each of the mentioned list. Remember, Noah knew the difference between the clean and unclean way before the law of Moses. The Bible even states that under the law identifying the clean from the unclean is connected with God's holiness.

> Leviticus 11: 45 "For I am the LORD that bringeth you up out of the land of Egypt, to be your God: ye shall therefore be holy, for I am holy.
>
> (46) This is the law of the beasts, and of the fowl, and of every living creature that moveth in the waters, and of every creature that creepeth upon the earth: (47) To make a difference between the unclean and the clean, and between the beast that may be eaten and the beast that may not be eaten."

Now with this understanding of sacrifices, let's look at the offerings that Cain and Abel brought before the LORD. Cain failed to bring a clean animal before the LORD, but Abel brought the best of the flock. Abel's offering was accepted while Cain's was rejected. Cain failed to follow God's method of approaching Him.

When Cain's offering was rejected, he then became very angry to the point of wrath. He became angry only AFTER his offering was rejected. There is no indication in the Bible that Cain brought the offering in anger. God would not accept the fruit offering and then Cain reacted with great anger. Cain did not come to worship before the LORD the way God had required. Cain came his own way which God rejected.

> Genesis 4:5 "But unto Cain and to his offer-
> ing he had not respect. And Cain was very
> wroth, and his countenance fell."

God then warned Cain what would happen if Cain did not
follow God's instruction of worship and coming before
Him. God told Cain, "If thou doest well, shalt thou not be
accepted?" The Bible clearly showed how Cain could do
well. The way was to bring the best of the flock of sheep
before the LORD. This was God's way as seen by the
actions of Noah, Job, Abraham, Isaac and then with Moses
and the law.

> Genesis 4:6 "And the LORD said unto Cain,
> Why art thou wroth? and why is thy counte-
> nance fallen? (7) If thou doest well, shalt
> thou not be accepted? and if thou doest not
> well, sin lieth at the door. And unto thee shall
> be his desire, and thou shalt rule over him."

God warned Cain that if he did not approach God the
correct way, sin was waiting to destroy him. Cain failed to
follow God's method and sin overtook him just as God said
would happen. In a moment of rage, Cain killed Abel, his
own brother. Cain followed the way of evil and was demon-
strating the conflict between the seed of the woman and the
seed of evil that continues to this day.

> Genesis 4:8 "And Cain talked with Abel his
> brother: and it came to pass, when they were
> in the field, that Cain rose up against Abel
> his brother, and slew him. (9) And the LORD
> said unto Cain, Where is Abel thy brother?

> And he said, I know not: Am I my brother's
> keeper? (10) And he said, What hast thou
> done? the voice of thy brother's blood crieth
> unto me from the ground."

The New Testament commentary on the story of Cain and
Abel is very interesting. The Apostle John writes that Cain's
work of bringing the fruit of the ground was evil and Abel's
was righteous. Abel by bringing a clean animal before the
LORD was made righteous. Cain was following the wicked
one, satan, and he killed his brother because of his evil
works. What Cain did by bringing the fruit was not just
wrong but evil!

> 1 John 3:12 "Not as Cain, who was of that
> wicked one, and slew his brother. And
> wherefore slew he him? Because his own
> works were evil, and his brother's righteous.
> (13) Marvel not, my brethren, if the world
> hate you."

The New Testament is in complete agreement with the Old
Testament that death is needed to pay the price for sin. God,
in the Old Testament, would only accept the burnt offerings
of clean animals for sin, and in the New Testament, He will
only accept the death of His Son to remit sin. To reject the
need for burnt offerings in the Old Testament and the death
of the Lord Jesus in the New Testament is to follow the way
of Cain and thus be rejected by God.

God will only accept His way to Him and that is through
the death and shed blood for sin of His Son, the Lord Jesus.
Cain tried his way and was outright rejected by the LORD.
Are you following the way of Cain or are you righteous like
Abel?

> Hebrews 9:28 "So Christ was once offered to bear the sins of many; and unto them that look for him shall he appear the second time without sin unto salvation."

One of the fundamental doctrines of Bible is that a vicarious death and blood atonement is needed to be cleansed of all sin. All the sacrifices for sin in the Hebrew Scriptures were types pointing to what the Messiah was going to accomplish. The fulfillment of the vicarious death for sin can be seen in Isaiah 53, when King Messiah, God's righteous servant, died for sin to justify many. Justify means to be made morally right or to cleanse. Through the Messiah, God's righteous Servant, sinful man was reconciled with the holy God of Israel.

> Leviticus 16:21 "And Aaron shall lay both his hands upon the head of the live goat, and confess over him all the **iniquities** of the children of Israel, and all their **transgressions** in all their **sins**, putting them upon the head of the goat, and shall send him away by the hand of a fit man into the wilderness:
>
> (22) And the goat shall bear upon him all their iniquities unto a land not inhabited: and he shall let go the goat in the wilderness."

CHAPTER TEN

For Behold the Stone
Engraved to Remove Iniquity

Zechariah 3:8 "Hear now, O Joshua the high
priest, thou, and thy fellows that sit before
thee: for they are men wondered at: for,
behold, I will bring forth my servant the
BRANCH. (9) For behold the stone that I
have laid before Joshua; upon one stone shall
be seven eyes: behold, I will engrave the
graving thereof, saith the LORD of hosts,
and I will remove the iniquity of that land in
one day."

Zechariah chapter three is a beautiful chapter full of
vivid imagery. The chapter opens with a vision. Joshua,
the high priest of Israel, is standing before the angel of the
LORD. This Joshua was the high priest who returned from
the Babylonian captivity and had no connection with the
Joshua at the time of Moses. The two Joshua's are about 800
years apart.

The vision begins with the high priest standing before

the angel of the LORD in a very unusual manner. In verse three, He is standing dressed in filthy garments. The high priest had a very special dress code which was carefully outlined by Moses. The high priest had to be dressed in a certain way to minister before the LORD.

The garments worn by him were called "holy garments." The holy garments were to be made for glory and beauty! The garments were made by special people whom God filled with the spirit of wisdom. The high priest had to wear these garments to stand before the LORD. The garments worn by the high priest were beautiful and holy and were essential in his ministry before the holy God of Israel.

The high priest dressed in filthy garments is shocking and needs special attention. This means he is barred from ministering to the LORD. This is the only time in the Bible that the high priest is described like this. The verses from Exodus showing the high priest's special dress code follow:

> Exodus 28:1 "And take thou unto thee Aaron thy brother, and his sons with him, from among the children of Israel, that he may minister unto me in the priest's office...(2) And thou shalt make holy garments for Aaron thy brother for glory and for beauty.
>
> (3) And thou shalt speak unto all that are wise hearted, whom I have filled with the spirit of wisdom, that they may make Aaron's garments to consecrate him, that he may minister unto me in the priest's office.
>
> (4) And these are the garments which they shall make; a breastplate, and an ephod, and a robe, and a broidered coat, a mitre, and a girdle: and they shall make holy garments for Aaron thy brother, and his sons, that he may minister unto me in the priest's office."

The head covering of the high priest also requires special interest. The covering was called a mitre or turban. It was part of the holy garments, the dress code, he needed to minister before the holy God of Israel. There was a pure gold band around the mitre. This band made the turban very special because on it was written: "HOLINESS TO THE LORD."

The high priest wearing his holy garments reflected God's holiness. When the people observed the high priest, they were to think of God's holiness. The mitre was the key to drawing everyone's attention to the holiness of God.

The high priest was always required to wear the mitre. He must wear this to be accepted before the LORD. The mitre was the most crucial of all the garments because it brought clearly to the attention of everyone the holiness of God. So any mention of the mitre needs careful attention as it focuses upon God's holiness. The verses about the mitre follow:

> Exodus 28:36 "And thou shalt make a plate of pure gold, and grave upon it, like the engravings of a signet, HOLINESS TO THE LORD. (37) And thou shalt put it on a blue lace, that it may be upon the mitre; upon the forefront of the mitre it shall be.
>
> (38) And it shall be upon Aaron's forehead, that Aaron may bear the iniquity of the holy things, which the children of Israel shall hallow in all their holy gifts; and it shall be always upon his forehead, that they may be accepted before the LORD."

In Zechariah 3:3,4, the angel of the LORD associates the high priest's filthy garments with iniquity. This means the high priest has no right to stand before the holy God of Israel. He should have been blocked from standing before the LORD because he no longer reflected God's holiness.

The filthy garments, including the mitre, would forfeit his ability to stand before God. What a dichotomy this creates. The high priest wearing filthy garments of iniquity while at the same time wearing a mitre with a gold band stating, Holiness to the LORD!

Joshua's garments are then changed, and a fair or clean mitre is put on his head. A clean mitre means that the high priest was now able to function and stand before the LORD. He was reflecting God's holiness. The Angel of the LORD said that he had caused the iniquity to pass from Joshua and to then clothe him with clean garments. The high priest's sins were now cleansed.

God does not tell at this point what happened to cause the iniquity to pass. The reason the filthy garments of iniquity could be changed to clean ones was also not mentioned at this time. The Angel of the LORD simply stated that He had caused the iniquity to pass and to clothe Joshua with clean garments. These verses follow:

> Zechariah 3:3 "Now Joshua was clothed with filthy garments, and stood before the angel. (4) And he answered and spake unto those that stood before him, saying, Take away the filthy garments from him. And unto him he said, Behold, I have caused thine iniquity to pass from thee, and I will clothe thee with change of raiment.
>
> (5) And I said, Let them set a fair mitre upon his head. So they set a fair mitre upon his head, and clothed him with garments. And the angel of the LORD stood by."

The high priest represented the nation before the holy God of Israel. In this chapter, he is seen in filthy garments because of both his sin and the nation's sin. This is a vivid picture of a sinful person standing before the holy God of Israel. It also shows that in an instant how a person filthy, because of iniquity can be made pure and clean before the LORD. The high priest was made clean by no action of his own. It was all God's doing that allowed the high priest's sin to pass and be dressed in clean garments.

The Bible gives special attention to the garments of the high priest on the Day of Atonement. On this day, he represents all of Israel before God. He offers the sacrifices and the atoning shed blood in the holy place for himself, his family, and the entire nation. He does this while wearing garments which the Bible calls, "Holy garments."

After this ritual is completed, he then changes his garments to clean ones and offers burnt offerings for himself and the people. The Bible, for a second time, carefully describes the garments of the high priest on the Day of Atonement. The importance of the high priest's garments follows:

> Leviticus 16:4 "He shall put on the holy linen coat, and he shall have the linen breeches upon his flesh, and shall be girded with a linen girdle, and with the linen mitre shall he be attired: these are holy garments; therefore shall he wash his flesh in water, and so put them on.
>
> (23) And Aaron shall come into the tabernacle of the congregation, and shall put off the linen garments, which he put on when he went into the holy place, and shall leave them there: (24) And he shall wash his flesh with water in the holy place, and put on his garments, and come forth, and offer his burnt offering, and the burnt offering of the people,

and make an atonement for himself, and for
the people."

On the Day of Atonement, when the high priest was dressed
properly and able to minister before the LORD, the people
were made clean from all their sin. The priest must wear
holy garments for the people to be clean from their sin
before the holy God of Israel. The garments must be clean,
as filthy garments would cause the people to remain unclean
before the LORD.

God showed His way to be clean from sin before Him.
The dress of the high priest was critical, and the shed blood
was needed to atone for the sin. It took the combination of
the high priest in proper garments plus the sacrifices and
sprinkling of the shed blood to cleanse the people of all their
iniquity, transgression and sin. The Scriptures to show this
follow:

> Leviticus 16:30 "For on that day shall the
> priest make an atonement for you, to cleanse
> you, that **ye may be clean from all your sins
> before the LORD**.
> (32) And the priest, whom he shall anoint,
> and whom he shall consecrate to minister in
> the priest's office in his father's stead, shall
> make the atonement, and shall put on the
> linen clothes, **even the holy garments:** (33)
> And he shall make an atonement for the holy
> sanctuary, and he shall make an atonement
> for the tabernacle of the congregation, and
> for the altar, and he shall make an atonement
> for the priests, and for all the people of the
> congregation."

According to Leviticus 16, for the iniquity to pass, there had to be a vicarious death and sprinkled blood in the holy of holies in the temple. But, herein lies the dilemma for the high priest. How can he offer the holy sacrifices needed to make him clean if he is wearing the filthy garments of iniquity? He must be wearing holy garments to offer the sacrifices on the Day of Atonement to make himself and the people clean before the holy God of Israel. He needs to be clean, but he cannot be made clean by himself because of his filthy garments of iniquity!

Notice it is the Angel of the LORD that causes the iniquity to pass from the high priest. Joshua had no part in being made clean as he just stood and both did and said nothing. This was all of God. If Joshua the high priest of Israel stands before the LORD in filthy garments of iniquity, what about the rest of us? How will our garments look standing before the holy God of Israel?

Behold My Servant the Branch

Zechariah 3:8 "Hear now, O Joshua the high priest, thou, and thy fellows that sit before thee: for they are men wondered at: for, behold, I will bring forth my servant the BRANCH.

(9) For behold the stone that I have laid before Joshua; upon one stone shall be seven eyes: behold, I will engrave the graving thereof, saith the LORD of hosts, and I will remove the iniquity of that land in one day."

In verse eight, God tells the prophet He is going to, "Bring forth my servant the Branch." We are not told at this point who the Branch is, but just that the Branch is God's servant. In the very next verse, the Branch is associated with a stone.

This is not a normal stone, but it has a supernatural element to it. The stone has seven eyes which means that it is all seeing, and it is representing something of the Branch. The Branch is going to be supernatural and not a mere man. Only God is all seeing.

God uses a stone to represent the Branch for several reasons. A stone is solid and does not change. It is strong and you can use it as a foundation to erect a building. It is enduring and will last over time. The pyramids built of stone by the Egyptians thousands of years ago are still standing today. A heavy stone can be used to crush objects. All of these descriptions can be applied to the Branch.

In verse nine, God is going to engrave this stone. This engraving is going to answer the question of why Joshua could be made holy before the LORD. This explains what caused the iniquity to pass from Joshua, and allowed him to be dressed in clean garments. The answer to being made clean is found by the engraving of the stone. This engraving will cleanse the people's sin in one day!

God is now showing how Joshua was changed from filthy garments of iniquity to clean ones, and why a clean mitre could be placed on his head. The ability for Joshua and the people to be cleansed from iniquity had to do with the Branch being engraved. The Hebrew word for engrave is *petch* (Strong's Concordance Number 6605). This is a very strong word that gives the connotation of being forcefully, broken open with violence. The engraving or carving is done by violence. This is what happened to the Branch.

It is critical to identify the Branch. Although verse eight does not indicate who the Branch is, other Scriptures reveal the identity. The Branch is a title for King Messiah. The word used here for Branch in Hebrew is *tzemach* (Strong's Concordance 6780.) Three of the prophets, Isaiah, Jeremiah and Zechariah, use the term the Branch to represent King Messiah. King Messiah is the Branch of David. He is David's

Son who will rule over all the nations in an eternal kingdom.

Jeremiah refers to the Branch as the King who will reign and will be called, "THE LORD OUR RIGHTEOUSNESS." He also called King Messiah the Branch of Righteousness. He will execute judgment and justice over the earth and will rule from Jerusalem. When He is ruling, there will be universal peace. Jeremiah used the word Branch to clearly describe King Messiah, the Son of David. This leaves no doubt that God's Servant the Branch is King Messiah. The verses from Jeremiah chapters 23 and 33 follow:

> Jeremiah 23:5 "Behold, the days come, saith the LORD, that I will raise unto David **a righteous Branch**, and a King shall reign and prosper, and shall execute judgment and justice in the earth. (6) In his days Judah shall be saved, and Israel shall dwell safely: and this is his name whereby he shall be called, THE LORD OUR RIGHTEOUSNESS."
>
> Jeremiah 33:15 "In those days, and at that time, will I cause **the Branch** of righteousness to grow up unto David; and he shall execute judgment and righteousness in the land. (16) In those days shall Judah be saved, and Jerusalem shall dwell safely: and this is the name wherewith she shall be called, The LORD our righteousness."

Zechariah uses the term the Branch a second time in chapter six. Like Jeremiah, he uses the Branch to illustrate King Messiah. In this illustration, Zechariah puts the crown of a king on Joshua the high priest and addresses him as the Branch. By doing this to Joshua, Zechariah is showing the Branch will be both King Messiah and the High Priest of Israel. He then states the Branch will build the temple of the

LORD. This is King Messiah's temple, and it will be built when He sets the kingdom up on earth. He will bear the glory as king and sit and rule upon the throne of David in the temple as both a king and priest.

It is so clear from Zechariah 6:11-13 that the Branch is a reference to the Messiah. What beautiful Scriptures these are to show the glory of the Branch, Israel's King Messiah! The prophet Zechariah gives such clear illustrations of the Branch and His ministry. These verses follow:

> Zechariah 6:12 "And speak unto him, saying, Thus speaketh the LORD of hosts, saying, Behold the man whose name is **The BRANCH**; and he shall grow up out of his place, and he shall build the temple of the LORD:
> (13) Even he shall build the temple of the LORD; and he shall bear the glory, and shall sit and rule upon his throne; and he shall be a priest upon his throne: and the counsel of peace shall be between them both."

The combination of both Jeremiah and Zechariah's use of the word Branch make it very clear this is King Messiah. It is the engraving/carving of King Messiah which will end iniquity in one day and allows the high priest to take off the filthy garments of iniquity and put on clean ones.

It was the carving of King Messiah for iniquity which allowed the Angel of the Lord to place a clean mitre on the head of Joshua. Joshua could do nothing on his own to be made clean. It was all the engraving of the Stone which allowed him to be made clean. God's Servant the Branch is King Messiah, the Son of David.

The prophet Isaiah ties in beautifully with Zechariah and the engraving of God's Servant the Branch for the removal of iniquity. Isaiah identifies the Branch as God's righteous Servant. He gives a vivid picture of what was the actual engraving of King Messiah and how it made Joshua clean from sin. The Branch would take the punishment for sin that mankind deserved. The engraving of the Stone was the bruises, stripes and punishment He took for sin.

> Isaiah 53:11 "He shall see of the travail of his soul, and shall be satisfied: by his knowledge shall my righteous servant justify many; for he shall bear their iniquities."

God's righteous Servant took all the punishment for iniquity even to the point of death. His soul was made an offering for sin as He bore our iniquities. The high priest could be made clean because the Branch paid the price for his sin. The engraving of the Stone was the reason the Angel of the Lord could put clean garments on Joshua. He could now wear the high priest's mitre because he was made holy by the death of the Branch, God's righteous Servant.

> Zechariah 3:4 "And he answered and spake unto those that stood before him, saying, Take away the filthy garments from him. And unto him he said, Behold, I have caused thine iniquity to pass from thee, and I will clothe thee with change of raiment."

The entire thrust of Isaiah chapter 53 is about the engraving of the Stone. It is a picture of King Messiah's first coming to pay the penalty for sin and enable us to be clean before the holy God of Israel. Remember the word engrave has the connotation of being violently ripped and torn open. This is the exact description of what happened to God's Servant.

Isaiah says God's Servant was smitten and afflicted. He

was wounded for transgressions, bruised for iniquities, and by His stripes there was healing. His soul was made an offering for sin and all iniquity was put on Him. He bore the sin of many. Notice the correlation between the engraving of God's Servant and sin. The Scriptures from Isaiah 53 to show the extent of the engraving follow:

> Isaiah 53:4 "Surely he hath borne our griefs, and carried our sorrows: yet we did esteem him stricken, smitten of God, and afflicted. (5) But he was wounded for our transgressions, he was bruised for our iniquities: the chastisement of our peace was upon him; and with his stripes we are healed.
>
> (6) All we like sheep have gone astray; we have turned every one to his own way; and the LORD hath laid on him the iniquity of us all.
>
> (8)...for he was cut off out of the land of the living: for the transgression of my people was he stricken. (10) Yet it pleased the LORD to bruise him; he hath put him to grief: when thou shalt make his soul an offering for sin...
>
> (11) He shall see of the travail of his soul, and shall be satisfied: by his knowledge shall my righteous servant justify many; for he shall bear their iniquities.
>
> (12) Therefore will I divide him a portion with the great, and he shall divide the spoil with the strong; because he hath poured out his soul unto death: and he was numbered with the transgressors; and he bare the sin of many, and made intercession for the transgressors."

Both Isaiah and Zechariah present a beautiful picture of how the Stone would be engraved to pay the penalty for sin.

Zechariah uses the Hebrew word for engraved one more time. He uses it to show that when the Branch comes to set up His kingdom there will be a fountain opened for sin and uncleanness. The Branch engraved became the opened fountain to cleanse from sin. The word opened in this verse is the same as engraved. This engraving provided all that is needed to be clean from sin and uncleanness. The verse follows:

> Zechariah 13:1 "In that day there shall be a fountain **opened** to the house of David and to the inhabitants of Jerusalem for sin and for uncleanness."

The New Testament gives more details about the engraving of the Branch for iniquity. The Lord Jesus, the King Messiah, was scourged, beaten and whipped by the Romans. The Romans used a whip with several lengths to it. At the end of each length were sharp objects like a piece of bone or metal. During the whipping, the sharp object would tear and rip the flesh.

He had a crown of thorns driven into His skull. He was beaten with rods and then taken to be crucified. During the crucifixion, huge nails where driven into the Lord Jesus' hands and feet. These nails were as large as railroad spikes. At the very end of the ordeal, a spear was driven into His side which caused both blood and water to flow from His body. The Scriptures to show the extent of the engraving of King Messiah follow:

> John 19:1 "Then Pilate therefore took Jesus, and scourged him. (2) And the soldiers plat-ted a crown of thorns, and put it on his head,

and they put on him a purple robe, (3) And said, Hail, King of the Jews! and they smote him with their hands.

(17) And he bearing his cross went forth into a place called the place of a skull, which is called in the Hebrew Golgotha: (18) Where they crucified him, and two others with him, on either side one, and Jesus in the midst.

(34) But one of the soldiers with a spear pierced his side, and forthwith came there out blood and water."

The blood and the water flowing from His side is very significant and is directly connected to King Messiah's temple and will be developed in the last chapter of the book.

The openings in the body of King Messiah were enormous. The nail holes in His hands and feet were large enough that a finger could be placed in them. Apparently, the spear that was driven into His side must have been turned and twisted. This action made a huge cavity because a hand could be placed in the wound. The engraving of the Branch was both deep and wide.

A tremendous personal sacrifice was made by the Lord Jesus so the high priest could be dressed in clean garments and stand in the very presence of the holy God of Israel. The Scriptures to show the enormous wounds in the Lord's body follow:

John 20:25 "The other disciples therefore said unto him, We have seen the Lord. But he said unto them, Except I shall see in his hands the print of the nails, and put my finger into the print of the nails, and thrust my hand into his side, I will not believe.

(27) Then saith he to Thomas, Reach hither

thy finger, and behold my hands; and reach hither thy hand, and thrust it into my side: and be not faithless, but believing."

The Coming of the Stone Cut Without Hands

Daniel 2:34 "Thou sawest till that a stone was cut out without hands, which smote the image upon his feet that were of iron and clay, and brake them to pieces. (35) Then was the iron, the clay, the brass, the silver, and the gold, broken to pieces together, and became like the chaff of the summer threshingfloors; and the wind carried them away, that no place was found for them: and the stone that smote the image became a great mountain, and filled the whole earth."

The Bible clearly uses the example of an engraved stone to show how King Messiah was going to cleanse Israel's high priest from sin. This was all accomplished at the first coming of the Lord Jesus. At His glorious second coming to set up His kingdom, the Bible also uses the imagery of a stone.

The first use of the stone was having it engraved for sin. For His second coming, the stone is an awesome crushing weight that destroys all the rebellious kingdoms of the world. The stone then becomes a huge mountain filling the entire earth.

The prophet Daniel interpreted a dream of the Babylonian King Nebuchadnezzar. This dream involved four world kingdoms that would arise and have power over Israel. These kingdoms were Babylon, Persia, Greece and Rome. The dream ends with a stone smashing a worldwide kingdom and then filling the entire earth. This last kingdom which is depicted as a, "Stone cut out without hands," is the kingdom of the Lord Jesus.

In both references to the Stone and the coming of King Messiah, there is a supernatural element. The engraved Stone had seven eyes showing the all seeing Branch. This time the Stone is made without hands. This means what is happening is all of God, and man has nothing to do with this event. The coming of the Stone to set up the kingdom will be supernatural.

At His second coming, He will smash this world kingdom and set up His own over the earth. The Hebrew word for stone in Daniel 2 is the same word used by Zechariah. Daniel sees King Messiah's second coming like a huge stone that crushes a world kingdom in rebellion against Him. The Lord Jesus then sets up His eternal kingdom which shall never be destroyed. Daniel's interpretation of the dream follows:

> Daniel 2:36 "This is the dream; and we will tell the interpretation thereof before the king.
>
> (44) And in the days of these kings shall the God of heaven set up a kingdom, which shall never be destroyed: and the kingdom shall not be left to other people, but it shall break in pieces and consume all these kingdoms, and it shall stand for ever.
>
> (45) Forasmuch as thou sawest that the stone was cut out of the mountain without hands, and that it brake in pieces the iron, the brass, the clay, the silver, and the gold; the great God hath made known to the king what shall come to pass hereafter: and the dream is certain, and the interpretation thereof sure."

Daniel adds more in chapter seven about the supernatural

coming of the Branch to set up His kingdom. He refers to the Stone in this prophecy as the Son of Man. When correlating the Scriptures, the Branch of David, the Stone, and the Son of Man are all the same person, King Messiah.

The "Stone cut without hands" in chapter seven is the Son of Man coming with the "clouds of heaven" to establish His kingdom on earth. The "clouds of Heaven" is a term used to describe the host of believers in heaven that return with the Lord Jesus. The host of believers is the church.

The Branch comes directly from heaven to establish His kingdom on earth. Everything about Israel's King Messiah is supernatural. The following are the Scriptures from Daniel 7 which show the awesome coming of the "Stone cut without hands" to establish His kingdom on earth:

> Daniel 7:13 "I saw in the night visions, and, behold, one like the Son of man came with the clouds of heaven, and came to the Ancient of days, and they brought him near before him.
> (14) And there was given him dominion, and glory, and a kingdom, that all people, nations, and languages, should serve him: his dominion is an everlasting dominion, which shall not pass away, and his kingdom that which shall not be destroyed."

King Messiah's reign is not by popular election. It is not by mandate from the United Nations or any other political organization. His rule is by God's decree. He will set the kingdom up directly under His authority and not the will of man. The coming of His kingdom is like a huge stone that crushes the nations in rebellion against the authority of God.

The Stone was engraved to pay the price for iniquity. This same Stone comes and crushes the nations in rebellion against God. They are not different stones but one stone with two different aspects.

How To Be Dressed in Clean Garments Before God

Lay aside the garments that are stained with sin
And be washed in the blood of the Lamb;
There's a fountain flowing for the soul unclean,
O be washed in the blood of the Lamb
(From the song: *Are You Washed in the Blood of the Lamb?*)

In Zechariah's vision, it was the engraving of the Stone which allowed for the iniquity to pass from the high priest and the filthy garments to be replaced with clean ones. Special garments have to be worn to be in God's presence.

The type of clothes a person wears is very telling. You can quickly determine a lot of information by the way a person dresses. You can tell if a person is in the military if he is wearing a uniform. The type of garments worn can identify many religious groups. A person's ethnic background can often be determined by the dress.

The same can be said for those that will be in heaven with the holy God of Israel. The Bible describes a wedding feast in heaven. This wedding is when the believers are brought into the presence of the Lord Jesus and a tremendous ceremony takes place. This event is called the marriage supper of the Lamb. Those that are present have to be wearing certain garments. These garments are very similar to those worn by the high priest on the Day of Atonement. When he entered into the holy of holies, the high priest wore these type garments.

The high priest wore clean linen garments when he came before the presence of the Holy God of Israel. At the marriage supper, the believers will also wear clean linen garments. These garments will be pure white linen and will reflect God's righteousness. The people must wear clean white garments in the presence of God.

These garments reflect the person's righteousness before God. No one will be allowed in God's presence with the filthy garments like Joshua the high priest wore. There must be a change of clothes exactly as the high priest went through. The Scriptures about the garments at the marriage supper follow:

> Revelation 19:7 "Let us be glad and rejoice, and give honour to him: for the marriage of the Lamb is come, and his wife hath made herself ready. (8) And to her was granted that she should be arrayed in fine linen, clean and white: for the fine linen is the righteousness of saints.
>
> (14) And the armies which were in heaven followed him upon white horses, clothed in fine linen, white and clean."

The Bible clearly tells how one can be dressed with clean garments and stand before God. It is the result of believing the Stone was engraved for sin. Zechariah shows how the engraving of the Stone caused the iniquity of the high priest to pass and allowed him to be clothed in clean garments. The New Testament shows that the engraving means to have your garments washed from the filth of sin in the shed blood of the Lord, Israel's King Messiah.

Those that are dressed in white robes of righteousness at the marriage supper have trusted in God's Stone that was engraved for their sin. The Branch's righteousness is now reflected in the clean white garments worn at the marriage supper. The people have been washed in the shed blood of the Lord Jesus and now are righteous before the holy God of Israel.

> Revelation 7:14 "And I said unto him, Sir, thou knowest. And he said to me, These are they which came out of great tribulation, and have washed their robes, and made them white in the blood of the Lamb."

I hope that your robes are clean, white, and pure. Will you stand before God in filthy garments of iniquity or will you stand in robes that have been washed by the blood of God's Lamb? He was the Stone that was engraved and caused the iniquity to pass.

> Are you washed in the blood
> In the soul-cleansing blood of the Lamb?
> Are your garments spotless? Are they white
> as snow?
> Are you washed in the blood of the Lamb?
> (Chorus: *Are You Washed in the Blood of the Lamb*)

Part Three:

King Messiah Coming to His Temple

CHAPTER ELEVEN

The Near Future: The Tale of Two Temples

"When ye therefore shall see the abomination of desolation, spoken of by Daniel the prophet, stand in the holy place, (whoso readeth, let him understand:) 16 Then let them which be in Judaea flee into the mountains" Matthew 24:15

The key to understanding Bible prophecy is the nation of Israel, Jerusalem and the Temple Mount in Jerusalem. In the Bible, the Temple Mount is called Mount Zion. The Temple Mount can be viewed as ground zero for Bible prophecy. An understanding of this prophecy of 2000 years ago leads right to the present time.

Just a few days before His crucifixion, the Lord Jesus spoke with His disciples on the Mount of Olives about the future of the temple and His second coming. The Mount of Olives is directly east of the temple and projects above it. From the top of this mountain, the disciples could look directly down on the temple as the Lord Jesus spoke to them. The temple was the focus of their attention.

He told them of the coming destruction of the temple and events to occur just prior to His return. His disciples asked Him three questions connected to the destruction of the temple. The questions the disciples asked were: What will be the circumstances surrounding the destruction of the temple; What will be the sign of His second coming; and What will be the end of the world? These questions are found in Matthew 24:1-3:

> Matthew 24:1 "And Jesus went out, and departed from the temple: and his disciples came to him for to show him the buildings of the temple. (2) And Jesus said unto them, See ye not all these things? verily I say unto you, There shall not be left here one stone upon another, that shall not be thrown down."
>
> (3) "And as he sat upon the mount of Olives, the disciples came unto him privately, saying, Tell us, when shall these things be? and what shall be the sign of thy coming, and of the end of the world?"

The answers to these questions are found in Matthew 24, Mark 13 and Luke 21. Luke gives the clearest answer to the circumstances surrounding the destruction of the temple. He warns that when the people see the armies gathering around Jerusalem, they would know the destruction of the temple was near. The surrounding of Jerusalem was the sign the temple was going to be destroyed.

> Luke 21:20 "And when ye shall see Jerusalem compassed with armies, then know that the desolation thereof is nigh."

Luke then went on to say that after the temple was destroyed, the Jews would be slaughtered and the survivors dispersed into all the nations. Jerusalem would be destroyed and under non-Jewish control for only a certain period of time, until God's plan was fulfilled. The Bible calls this non-Jewish control of Jerusalem the time of the Gentiles.

> Luke 21:24 "And they shall fall by the edge of the sword, and shall be led away captive into all nations: and Jerusalem shall be trodden down of the Gentiles, until the times of the Gentiles be fulfilled."

Luke 21:24 has been in effect from the destruction of Jerusalem and the temple by the Roman armies in 70 AD until today. Remember, this destruction is not an indefinite time period. It will come to an end. Matthew 24 picks up at the end of the times of the Gentiles with the events to occur directly before the second coming of Jesus.

Matthew warns that just before the Lord's return there were going to be worldwide wars, famines, earthquakes and pestilence. He then gives the key to the sign of the second coming. He told that something dreadful would happen in the temple. This event is called the "abomination of desolation" which was written by Daniel the prophet. This event in the holy place of the temple would be the key event to recognize that His coming was near. The people living at this time were given instruction to flee.

This event in the holy place would trigger the awesome worldwide events that would bring about the near destruction of mankind. The key to the events leading to the second coming of the Lord Jesus has to do with the temple in Jerusalem. Luke reported that the temple was going to be destroyed, but Matthew shows that there will be a temple standing just prior to the Lord's return. These verses follow:

> Matthew 24:15 "When ye therefore shall see the abomination of desolation, spoken of by Daniel the prophet, stand in the holy place, (whoso readeth, let him understand:) (16) Then let them which be in Judaea flee into the mountains"
>
> (21) "For then shall be great tribulation, such as was not since the beginning of the world to this time, no, nor ever shall be. (22) And except those days should be shortened, there should no flesh be saved: but for the elect's sake those days shall be shortened."

Luke reports the destruction of the temple, yet Matthew shows that one will be standing just prior to the Lord's return. This means that the temple, or some form of it, has to be rebuilt at the end of the age sometime prior to the second coming.

Matthew reports that the holy place of the temple is going to be the scene of something horrific. He does not say exactly what this is. The prophet Daniel and the apostle Paul write about what is going to happen. Daniel shows that Israel is going to make a covenant for seven years with a world ruler, but half way through, this world ruler is going to break it. The covenant involves the Jews being able to offer sacrifices in the temple, but the abomination of desolation is going to end the sacrifices.

Paul writes that a person of unspeakable evil is going to go into the most holy place of the temple and declare that he is God. The abomination of desolation is when a world ruler goes into the rebuilt temple in Jerusalem and declares that he is God. This will be the event that the Bible warns will occur immediately prior to the awesome second coming of the Lord Jesus. The verses to show this follow:

Daniel 9:27 "And he shall confirm the covenant with many for one week: and in the midst of the week he shall cause the sacrifice and the oblation to cease, and for the over-spreading of abominations he shall make it desolate, even until the consummation, and that determined shall be poured upon the desolate."

2 Thessalonians 2:3 "Let no man deceive you by any means: for that day shall not come, except there come a falling away first, and that man of sin be revealed, the son of perdition; (4) Who opposeth and exalteth himself above all that is called God, or that is worshipped; so that he as God sitteth in the temple of God, showing himself that he is God."

The person that Paul identifies as sitting in the temple of God is called by various names in the Bible. Daniel calls him the beast, Daniel 7:11. John refers to him as both the anti-christ and the beast, 1 John 2:18, Revelation 19:20. Paul calls him the son of perdition and man of sin.

Luke wrote that the destruction of Jerusalem would have a specific time period, and prophet after prophet in the Bible wrote about the rebirth of the nation of Israel and Jerusalem as the capital. The prophet Ezekiel, for example, writes about the restoration of the nation.

Ezekiel 37:21 "And say unto them, Thus saith the Lord GOD; Behold, I will take the children of Israel from among the heathen, whither they be gone, and will gather them on every side, and bring them into their own land:"

After being destroyed as a nation for 1900 years, Israel was reborn as a nation in 1948, just as the prophets wrote would happen. The prophets wrote about both the literal destruction of the nation and the literal restoration of the nation.

In 1967 during the Six-day War, Israel captured East Jerusalem. This is the section of Jerusalem where the Temple Mount is located. For the first time since 70 AD, Jerusalem was once again the capital of the nation of Israel. This is nearly a 1900 year gap. The times of the Gentiles, just as the Lord Jesus said would happen, were coming to an end!

The restoration of Israel and the rebuilding of the temple are to be viewed as literal. There is nothing in the Bible to indicate otherwise and current events show this to be literal. The following Scripture shows that Jerusalem was going to be restored as the capital of Israel:

> Zechariah 12:6 "In that day will I make the governors of Judah like an hearth of fire among the wood, and like a torch of fire in a sheaf; and they shall devour all the people round about, on the right hand and on the left: and **Jerusalem shall be inhabited again in her own place, even in Jerusalem.**"

On September 28, 2000, fierce fighting broke out in Jerusalem over the Temple Mount. This fighting expanded to a low-grade war between Israel and the Palestinians. This fighting has the possibility to escalate into a regional war using weapons of mass destruction that could destroy entire nations. Remember, the Temple Mount is ground zero of Bible prophecy.

All this is very important because just prior to the second coming of the Lord Jesus, a temple will be built in Jerusalem. This temple will not be the one from which the true King Messiah will rule. This temple will be built along the lines of the Solomon's temple and will not be King Messiah's temple as described in Ezekiel 40-48.

The Apostle John wrote in the Book of Revelation that a temple would be built just before the second coming of the Lord Jesus. There is no doubt that, in the near future, Israel will build a temple on Mount Zion in Jerusalem. The rebirth of the nation of Israel was literal. Jerusalem being the capital of this state was literal. The rebuilding of the temple on Mount Zion is also literal.

> Revelation 11:1,2 "And there was given me a reed like unto a rod: and the angel stood, saying, Rise, and measure the temple of God, and the altar, and them that worship therein. But the court which is without the temple leave out, and measure it not; for it is given unto the Gentiles: and the holy city shall they tread under foot forty and two months."

In the near future, two temples are going to be built. The one just prior to the second coming of the Lord Jesus will be similar in design to the previous temples and the Tabernacle in the Wilderness. This temple will be destroyed at the second coming. The next will be built after the Lord's second coming. This temple will be built radically different from all the previous temples because it will be built, not under the law of Moses, but under the New Covenant.

In certain Jewish and Christian circles, there is an increasing fervor about the building of a temple on the site in Jerusalem where the previous temples stood. In anticipation of the coming temple, the Temple Institute in Jerusalem is preparing the items needed to furnish this temple. These items include the menorah, table of shew bread, altar of incense, high priest garments and many other temple related items. This temple will be built. The question is how soon?

How to identify the Messiah's Temple

It is very important to be able to identify the temple from which the true King Messiah, the Lord Jesus, will be seated on the throne of David. The temple built before His coming will be used by the beast or anti-christ to proclaim that he is God. A knowledge of the temples will prevent anyone in mistaking the temple built on the present day location of Mount Zion as being the one for the true King Messiah.

The easiest way to recognize the true temple is that awesome geographical changes have to take place in the area around Jerusalem. There has to be a massive earthquake that will literally split the Mount of Olives from the east to the west. This earthquake will produce a great valley, as half the mountains will move north and the other half south. This will produce a great valley several miles wide!

> Zechariah 14:4 "And his feet shall stand in that day upon the mount of Olives, which is before Jerusalem on the east, and the mount of Olives shall cleave in the midst thereof toward the east and toward the west, and there shall be a very great valley; and half of the mountain shall remove toward the north, and half of it toward the south."

This area around Jerusalem has to be leveled and then raised up as a high mountain or plain. The temple will then be built on this high plain. Ezekiel reported the temple and Jerusalem would be built on a very high mountain. While Zechariah said it would be leveled and turned into a plain. The temple grounds will be a square, approximately 1.5 miles on each side that would be impossible to fit in modern Jerusalem.

> Zechariah 14:10 "All the land shall be

turned as a plain from Geba to Rimmon south of Jerusalem: and it shall be lifted up, and inhabited in her place, from Benjamin's gate unto the place of the first gate, unto the corner gate, and from the tower of Hananeel unto the king's winepresses."
Ezekiel 40:2 "In the visions of God brought he me into the land of Israel, and set me upon a very high mountain, by which was as the frame of a city on the south."

Another sure way to recognize the true temple is to understand the second coming of the Lord Jesus. The true temple is going to be built after His coming, not before. The Lord is coming in awesome glory and power. His glory will be brighter than the sun. He is returning as awesome events are happening in the heavens. The powers of the heaven will be shaken at His return.

Matthew 24:29 "Immediately after the tribulation of those days shall the sun be darkened, and the moon shall not give her light, and the stars shall fall from heaven, and the powers of the heavens shall be shaken:
(30) And then shall appear the sign of the Son of man in heaven: and then shall all the tribes of the earth mourn, and they shall see the Son of man coming in the clouds of heaven with power and great glory."

He is not coming as the head of any world organization or as an elected ruler. He is coming in supernatural power in awesome glory. Any world ruler that comes to power naturally, as the head of a world power or organization, does not fulfill the second coming of the Lord Jesus.

> 2 Thessalonians 1:7 "And to you who are troubled rest with us, when the Lord Jesus shall be revealed from heaven with his mighty angels, (8) In flaming fire taking vengeance on them that know not God, and that obey not the gospel of our Lord Jesus Christ…"

At the Lord's return, He will destroy all the armies of the nations that have gathered to destroy Jerusalem. These armies will be destroyed supernaturally by the brightness of His glory and not by any man-made means. After the destruction of these armies, then He will build His house.

> Ezekiel 39:21 "And I will set my glory among the heathen, and all the heathen shall see my judgment that I have executed, and my hand that I have laid upon them."

He will then set His magnificent temple in Jerusalem and rule in His glory from Mount Zion. This is the true King Messiah sitting on His throne of David in the temple. The Bible calls it the throne of glory.

> Matthew 25:31 "When the Son of man shall come in his glory, and all the holy angels with him, then shall he sit upon the throne of his glory: (32) And before him shall be gathered all nations: and he shall separate them one from another, as a shepherd divideth his sheep from the goats:"

The last way to tell the true Messiah's temple is by the articles in the temple. King Messiah's temple will have His throne in the most holy place. In the holy place will be a small table located just in front of the entrance to the most holy place. Just outside the entrance to the temple will be the altar of sacrifice. King Messiah's temple will have just three articles in it: the throne, small table and altar of sacrifice.

The temple before the coming of King Messiah will have all the articles described under the law of Moses. There will be an altar of sacrifice, brazen laver, menorah, table of show bread, altar of incense, veil of separation and the Ark of the Covenant. In addition, this temple will have a high priest like Aaron. This temple will not have the throne of David in it.

With the understanding of the Scriptures, it is impossible to be confused about the true identity of King Messiah's temple. The rebuilding of the temple under the law of Moses is the sure sign that the period of time before the second coming of Jesus Christ is near. It is not the sign that He is going to reign from this temple. The beast, anti-christ, or man of sin as he is called will first have to go into this temple and proclaim that he is God. This is the abomination of desolation which will be the sure sign of the second coming of the true King Messiah to set up His temple.

The beast is coming with all lying signs and wonders. He will have some level of supernatural occult power. Do not be fooled into thinking this ruler, with lying signs and wonders, is the second coming of the King Messiah. The Lord Jesus is coming in flaming fire in full manifestation of His glory. The contrast of the anti-christ with the true King Messiah follows:

The false messiah or anti-christ:
> 2 Thessalonians 2:8 "And then shall that Wicked be revealed, whom the Lord shall consume with the spirit of his mouth, and shall destroy with the brightness of his coming:
> (9) Even him, whose coming is after the

working of Satan with all power and signs and lying wonders, (10) And with all deceivableness of unrighteousness in them that perish; because they received not the love of the truth, that they might be saved."

The true King Messiah:

Matthew 24:29 "Immediately after the tribulation of those days shall the sun be darkened, and the moon shall not give her light, and the stars shall fall from heaven, and the powers of the heavens shall be shaken:

(30) And then shall appear the sign of the Son of man in heaven: and then shall all the tribes of the earth mourn, and they shall see the Son of man coming in the clouds of heaven with power and great glory. (31) And he shall send his angels with a great sound of a trumpet, and they shall gather together his elect from the four winds, from one end of heaven to the other."

CHAPTER TWELVE

The Far Future: No Temple

"And I saw no temple therein: for the Lord God Almighty and the Lamb are the temple of it." Revelation 21:22

The Bible gives details of what will happen in the far future. The Lord's reign in Jerusalem will be for 1000 years. At the end of this time period, satan will be loosed to once again test the hearts of the people. Those who have lived under the reign of the Lord, but have been secretly rebelling against His authority, will join together in an organized attempt to dethrone King Messiah. This rebellion will end quickly with swift judgment. God will send fire upon the rebellion and end it. This will be mankind's final rebellion.

Revelation 20:7 "And when the thousand years are expired, Satan shall be loosed out of his prison,

(8) "And shall go out to deceive the nations which are in the four quarters of the earth, Gog and Magog, to gather them together to battle: the number of whom is as the sand of

> the sea. (9) And they went up on the breadth
> of the earth, and compassed the camp of the
> saints about, and the beloved city: and fire
> came down from God out of heaven, and
> devoured them."

Even with ideal conditions under the rule of the Lord Jesus, man will still have the tendency to challenge God's authority. During the reign of King Messiah, willful sin will not be tolerated. He will reign with a rod of iron and the sinner will come under the curse of God. With this final testing of man, the people in rebellion will come under the curse as they are consumed by fire from heaven.

Immediately after this, God initiates the judgment of mankind for all those who are not under the salvation that God provided through the Lord Jesus. This is called the Great White Throne judgment and is found in Revelation 20:11-15. This is the judgment for eternal damnation. It is also called the second death.

> Revelation 20:11 "And I saw a great white
> throne, and him that sat on it, from whose
> face the earth and the heaven fled away; and
> there was found no place for them.
> (14) "And death and hell were cast into the
> lake of fire. This is the second death. (15)
> And whosoever was not found written in the
> book of life was cast into the lake of fire."

After this judgment, God merges heaven and earth into one. The New Jerusalem, which is referred to as a city from God, is more like a country in size. It is about 1500 miles by 1500 miles and very high. This city rests on earth and becomes the home for the Lord Jesus and the redeemed of all time. The verses to show this follow:

> Revelation 21:1 "And I saw a new heaven
> and a new earth: for the first heaven and the
> first earth were passed away; and there was
> no more sea. (2) And I John saw the holy
> city, new Jerusalem, coming down from God
> out of heaven, prepared as a bride adorned
> for her husband."

The New Jerusalem will be spectacular in colors and beauty. It will be made up of layers upon layers of beautiful precious stones and minerals. This city will have layers of incredible colors and combinations with different shades of colors. Think of the beauty of this city when the glory of God shines through it! God's glory shining through the colors of Jerusalem will be the light of the universe.

> Revelation 21:11 "Having the glory of God:
> and her light was like unto a stone most
> precious, even like a jasper stone, clear as
> crystal...(19) And the foundations of the wall
> of the city were garnished with all manner of
> precious stones. The first foundation was
> jasper; the second, sapphire; the third, a chal-
> cedony; the fourth, an emerald..."

There will be no temple in the New Jerusalem. When God creates a new heaven and a new earth, it will not contain a temple. The temple will be replaced by the very presence of the Lord Jesus in His full glory. The new earth will not have a sun for light. Instead, the glory of King Messiah will light the heavens and the earth.

Think of the magnificent beauty when the entire universe is given light by the glory of God shining through the New Jerusalem. All the incredible colors of the New Jerusalem will magnify God's glory as His light shines through it. There will be no temple as there will be no more need for one.

> Revelation 21:22 "And I saw no temple therein: for the Lord God Almighty and the Lamb are the temple of it. (23) And the city had no need of the sun, neither of the moon, to shine in it: for the glory of God did lighten it, and the Lamb is the light thereof."

What will remain in the New Jerusalem will be the throne of God. God will sit openly on the throne of David in the midst of His people for ever and ever. Under the law of Moses, no one could look directly into God's face. However, in the New Jerusalem under the New Covenant of the Lord Jesus, everyone can behold the face of God.

> Revelation 22:3 "And there shall be no more curse: but the throne of God and of the Lamb shall be in it; and his servants shall serve him: (4) And they shall see his face; and his name shall be in their foreheads."

What an awesome reconciliation King Messiah accomplished with the New Covenant! Because of the death and shed blood of the Lord Jesus, redeemed man will be able to dwell openly in the presence of the holy God of Israel and look directly into His face. God will be our Father and He will refer to those in heaven with Him as, "my son." It does not get any better than having God call you His son.

> Revelation 21:7 "He that overcometh shall inherit all things; and I will be his God, and he shall be my son."

CHAPTER THIRTEEN

The Witness of the Water and the Blood

"And there are three that bear witness in earth, the Spirit, and the water, and the blood: and these three agree in one." 1 John 5:8

When the Lord Jesus died on the cross and shed His blood to pay the price for sin, the Bible says that blood and water flooded from His side. A Roman soldier drove a spear deep into King Messiah's side to make sure that He was dead. The Apostle John, who was an eyewitness to this event, reported that blood and water poured out of the wound. The blood and water were a witness to His death and the beginning of the New Covenant.

John 19:34,35 "But one of the soldiers with a spear pierced his side, and forthwith came there out blood and water. And he that saw it bare record, and his record is true: and he knoweth that he saith true, that ye might believe."

173

The Apostle John reported that there are three that bear witness in the earth. These are the Holy Spirit, the water and the blood. The water and the blood are directly related to the death of the Lord Jesus on the cross. The pouring of the blood and water from the wound bears witness to His finished work on the cross.

The Spirit of God bears witness to mankind to the water and the blood that the Lord Jesus shed at His death. God's Holy Spirit bearing witness in a person's heart is what leads to trusting in Jesus as Savior.

> 1 John 5:8 "And there are three that bear witness in earth, the Spirit, and the water, and the blood: and these three agree in one."

When the Lord Jesus reigns from His magnificent house in Jerusalem, there will be a witness in the earth to the blood and the water. His house will be the witness at that time. The outside of His temple will have the witness of the blood on it.

> Ezekiel 45:19 "And the priest shall take of the blood of the sin offering, and put it upon the posts of the house, and upon the four corners of the settle of the altar, and upon the posts of the gate of the inner court."

This will be the witness for all to see that King Messiah shed His blood to pay the price for sin. What a witness this will be to what the Lord Jesus had to do for man's redemption!

> Colossians 1:20 "And, having made peace through the blood of his cross, by him to reconcile all things unto himself; by him, I say, whether they be things in earth, or things in heaven."

The temple will also bear witness to the water that flowed from His side. Messiah's house will be the source of flowing water. The water of life will flow from the sanctuary, under the foundation of the house, past the altar of sacrifice and out of the temple. It will flow like a mighty river, giving life to all that are touched by it.

> Ezekiel 47:1 "Afterward he brought me again unto the door of the house; and, behold, waters issued out from under the threshold of the house eastward: for the forefront of the house stood toward the east, and the waters came down from under from the right side of the house, at the south side of the altar."
>
> (12) "And by the river upon the bank thereof, on this side and on that side, shall grow all trees for meat, whose leaf shall not fade, neither shall the fruit thereof be consumed: it shall bring forth new fruit according to his months, because their waters they issued out of the sanctuary: and the fruit thereof shall be for meat, and the leaf thereof for medicine."

The Holy Spirit in that day will bear witness to the people of the blood and the water of King Messiah just as He does in the earth today. The everlasting gospel of the shed blood of the Lord Jesus will never fade away. God will always have His witness to the New Covenant that was sealed by water and blood. The temple will be that witness.

The waters of life that will flow from the future temple in Jerusalem are flowing now for the person who is thirsty for God. Now is the time for all to accept the witness of the blood and the water in your life. Whoever repents of sin and confesses the Lord Jesus as their Savior comes under the

New Covenant. God offers the water of life freely to all who will trust His King Messiah for eternal life.

The water of eternal life is flowing right now as a mighty river for all who are thirsty. All who repent and confess Jesus as Savior and Lord come under the witness of the water and the blood. They have assurance of eternal life with God.

> Revelation 22:17 "And the Spirit and the bride say, Come. And let him that heareth say, Come. And let him that is athirst come. And whosoever will, let him take the water of life freely."

The world is now hurtling toward the darkest time in history. Incredible wars are going to be fought over Jerusalem that will result in the killing of a third of mankind. A false christ (messiah) will rise to power and deceive multitudes to damnation. A temple will be built on Mount Zion that will be defiled by this false messiah. All this will all occur immediately prior to the greatest time for mankind.

The greatest time for mankind will begin with the awesome second coming of the Lord Jesus with His Church, the "clouds of heaven," to establish His kingdom. King Messiah will build His magnificent temple in Jerusalem that will be a beacon for His glory. The earth will be blessed. Peace will reign on earth. All the nations will come to Jerusalem to worship the King seated on the throne of David in His holy house.

We cry like the apostle John did some 1900 years ago, "Even so, Come Lord Jesus," Revelation 22:20.

Index of Scriptures

Printed in the United States
38874LVS00003B/1-51

9 781597 813006